Endorsements

John Alarid's *My Prison Became a Palace* is not only critical in its timeliness, dealing directly with the opioid crisis through the story of his own addiction and incarceration, but also universal in its application. Whether your personal prison is material, spiritual or psychological in nature, your future is not defined by your past or present heartbreaks, setbacks and failures. This book will give you eyes to see that God is poised to turn your greatest struggles into your very own redemption story and John is living proof of how true this can be for all of us

Rev. Samuel Rodriguez
President, National Hispanic Christian Leadership Conference
Lead Pastor, New Season
Author of *Be Light*
www.pastorsam.com

My Prison Became a Palace will inspire and challenge you. From hopeless circumstances to profound experiences with the living God, John Alarid takes us on a captivating journey into God's grace and calling. It is my personal privilege to call him a friend and ministry partner.

Dr. James T. Bradford
Pastor, Central Assembly of God (Springfield, MO)
General Secretary, The General Council of the Assemblies of God

The life story of John Alarid is one that will teach us all a lot about pain. His story is defined by a tremendous perspective on how God is working in our struggles even though much of the time we don't realize it. I'm so thankful for my friend John and thankful that God chose to work in him and through him because he is now able to do so much to help people—and I believe that reading this book will be one of the greatest experiences you've had.

Dino Rizzo
Executive Director, Association of Related Churches (ARC)
Associate Pastor, Church of the Highlands (Birmingham, AL)
Author of *Servolution*

This book is a vibrant example of the mercy, grace, and power of God. John's story is one that will leave you in awe of God's continual pursuit of the lost and His ability to radically change a life!

John Lindell
Lead Pastor, James River Church (Ozark, MO)

As I read John Alarid's personal story of rebellion and depravity to finding grace and a call to proclaim the hope he himself had found in Christ, I couldn't help but think of John Newton, the depraved slave trader who gave us the most widely sung hymn of all—"Amazing Grace." I thought of Newton's epitaph, which reads: "John Newton, clerk, once an infidel and libertine, a servant of slaves in Africa, was by the rich mercy of our Lord and Saviour Jesus Christ, preserved, restored, pardoned, and appointed to preach the faith he had long labored to destroy." John Alarid's story reminds us that God's amazing grace continues to rescue broken lives and use them to proclaim hope to those who some would declare beyond reach.

Carol Taylor, PhD
President, Evangel University

From the depths of crime, drug addiction and immense personal pain, John Alarid's story will at times seem overwhelming to the reader. It is, however, a testimony to a powerful reality. God's redeeming and transforming power is infinitely greater than any other power on earth. *My Prison became a Palace* is an incredible story of divine grace. It reminds us that while the power of sin is great, it need not lead to death because God is able to deliver no matter how deep life's despair. John's redemption story is one that can give hope to all who find themselves in the most hopeless circumstances. When life appears to be all but over, God is still there with arms wide open to save, heal, restore and transform. John's testimony is a reminder that we serve a living God, one that is infinitely able to take a life that is "nothing" and make it into something of incredible meaning that can leave an impact on countless others.

Michael Jaffe, DMin
Professor of Preaching and Church Leadership,
Evangel University and Assemblies of God
Theological Seminary

John Alarid is definitely a true trophy of God's grace. When you begin reading his new book, *My Prison Became a Palace*, you won't be able to stop until you have finished it. You will experience the pain of satanic destruction; the power of the prayers of Godly parents; and the transformational presence of Jesus Christ, even in solitary confinement. Satan used John to lead many into bondage; now God is anointing him to help many receive their freedom. I encourage you to gift this book to anyone needing deliverance from any addiction.

Dr. Alton Garrison
Assistant General Superintendent,
The General Council of the Assemblies of God

John Alarid's book is the story of how God's relentless love pursued a man all the way to a lonely prison cell, in order to have mercy upon him. John, a modern day prodigal son, was running from God until he reached a place where for five months he found himself with almost no human contact, and only a Bible to read. In that place, a rebel found repentance; a sinner found the Savior; a prodigal found the Father; and a prisoner found a palace. My wife and I have worshipped several times with the congregation at Freedom City Church in Springfield, Missouri. When you walk into the building, you encounter an atmosphere of God's love and presence, and you meet people with amazing stories of transformation. When you hear John Alarid preach, you know that hope has made a comeback to the streets of North Springfield.

Dennis Rivera
Director of Hispanic Relations,
The General Council of the Assemblies of God

This book is the story of one man's journey out of darkness into the marvelous light. I first met John when he entered our recovery home at Victory Outreach in Phoenix. After graduating from the home, he served in leadership at the recovery homes. Later he graduated the Urban Training Center in Los Angeles and served as a missionary to Manila, Philippines. He went on to finish advanced degrees and plant churches. John is truly a treasure out of darkness. I am proud to call him my spiritual son.

Tony Garcia
Senior Pastor, Victory Outreach (Phoenix, AZ)
Regional Pastor, Victory Outreach International

My Prison Became a Palace is *The Cross and the Switchblade* of this generation.

Dr. Rod Parsley
Lead Pastor, World Harvest Church

My friend John Alarid is not only a *miracle*, but he is a *missionary*. For a number of years he served us well in Manila, Philippines as an urban missionary, reaching and training young leaders. He has never forgotten where he came from and continues to radically reach out to the lost and hurting of society. His story is one that will inspire you and provide light to anyone who has ever been told that their situation is hopeless. John is proof that God is still reaching into darkness and raising up the foolish things of the world. To God be the glory!

Pastor Al Valdez
Board of Elders, Victory Outreach International
Pastor, Victory Outreach Church (San Diego, CA)

When you read John's story, you are not just reading the story of his life. You are reading the story of God's power and grace. To see someone's life changed as radically as John Alarid's truly gives hope to everyone breathing air today. I pray God encourages your life through the honesty and transformational history of this amazing story of grace.

Jeff Leake
Lead Pastor, Allison Park Church (Allison Park, PA)

This book is a great story of redemption. It is an example that shows it does not matter how far you wander, the Father is still looking for you. He can rescue you and save you. John Alarid reaches out to the downtrodden and disenfranchised because he has been there. This book will encourage you to never give up; those who do are walking away from the Lord's grace.

Manuel Cordero
Senior Director of Chaplaincy Ministries,
The General Council of the Assemblies of God

The book you are holding in your hand is a powerful story of hope and redemption that will serve as a reminder of the faithfulness of God. While the details may be different, John's story of wandering, doubt, hopelessness and pain is in many ways common to us all, and if you look closely you'll find a piece of your story here as well. As you walk with John through hurt to hope, you'll be inspired and encouraged by the grace and love of God and the lengths He goes to pursue us. This is a story of hope, and you won't want to put it down!

Chris Railey
Senior Director of Leadership and Church Development,
The General Council of the Assemblies of God

John Alarid's story deserves to be heard. Any person whose life is marked by tragedy who reads *My Prison became a Palace* will quickly identify with John Alarid's story. This is not soft-sell religion, but "in your face" truth-telling about what can happen when you encounter Jesus Christ face-to-face. John Alarid's story demonstrates that when you meet Christ, your old life doesn't rule anymore, and a new reality has dawned. John's chain-breaking experience is the foundation of a vibrant dream to reach a city where there is a church on every corner, but thousands remain captive to self-destructive violence. John is the real deal and his story will remind you that whatever your tragedy may be, hope is never in short supply because Jesus is alive and well!

Byron D. Klaus
President (1999-2015), Assemblies of God Theological
Seminary (Springfield, MO)

In what is his first book, *My Prison Became a Palace*, Pastor John Caleb Alarid sets the tone for conveying his personal "story" of God's amazing grace with these words: "My prison became a palace. My dungeon was filled with light. I felt what were like waves of electric liquid love flowing over me for five months."

From the very outset, Pastor John shares the challenging "before" of his life's journey without knowing the God who loved him and desired to redeem him from his rebellion, sin, and trials of life through the powerful and life-changing good news of his Son Jesus. Pastor John's "after" experience ultimately came as God relentlessly pursued him through the course of his ongoing self-defeating lifestyle that included taking and then dealing hardcore drugs in an endeavor to find meaning. Yet, from that pit of despair, God remained faithful in finally breaking through John's downward spiral to prevail marvelously in this prodigal's life.

His unbelievable story is not told to glamorize any dark exploits, but to reveal the wonder of God's larger love story that calls everyone, regardless of circumstances, to full awareness by the Spirit and a relationship with Jesus Christ. I recommend *My Prison Became a Palace* for reading and sharing with those who feel hopeless and lost—who need their prison transformed to a palace.

Rich Guerra
Superintendent, SoCal Network (Pastor Rich oversees a
network of over 400 churches in California)

God is in the business of redeeming the broken. He always has been. John Alarid is a living example of God's transformational power. His book, *My Prison Became a Palace*, will satisfy your craving for some hope in tough times.

Doug Clay
General Superintendent,
The General Council of the Assemblies of God

John Alarid is a gifted speaker and author. His story—and more importantly, his deep passionate faith—has the potential to change lives. John shares his life experiences to provide a glimpse into a dark world many people are drawn to for quick money, and a perception of fulfillment. John dispels that myth with clarity and provides a clear path to true peace. He is both gentle, yet "Goliath like" in his mission to save each person that crosses his path.

Elizabeth Stanosheck
Prison Fellowship Area Director

I am always spiritually encouraged when I read the miraculous story of how God touched the lives of men and women that have survived incarceration. This amazing story of how God touched the life of someone that had reached rock bottom will touch your heart. This truly reflects the truth of C. S. Lewis's statement that the "Hound of Heaven will never give up on us". This is an amazing story of a man who in his depth of depravity dropped to his knees and asked Christ into his life. In his short life as a new Christian, John has already touched thousands of lives for the kingdom. This should be required reading for anyone struggling with incarceration or families who have given up on their loved ones. I am proud to call John and Hannah my brother and sister in Christ.

Captain Tom Maxwell,
U.S. Navy retired,
Director Emeritus, Prison Fellowship Missouri

At a time when our nation is suffering from the worst plague of addiction in our history, here is a timely story of recovery and transformation out of the depths of drugs with all their effects. It began when the seeds leading to addiction were planted early in a disruptive childhood followed by bad choices as a young adult.

My Prison became a Palace is a well-told, gripping account of a young man's descent into the hell-hole of drug addiction, drug selling, prison and all that goes with such a lifestyle. Yet in it all was the over-shadowing grace of God. This is an amazing life story of change, transformation and hope. I highly recommend this book. It will inspire the reader; more importantly it is a modern "sign and wonder" that addiction does not have to be a life sentence. If you or a loved one has a life-controlling problem, read this book. It can help change a life.

Don Wilkerson
Co-founder of Teen Challenge and Times Square Church
Founder of Global Teen Challenge

What a beautiful picture of God's grace John has painted with this book! As I see John's life now, it is one of integrity, purity, and total commitment to God. It is hard to fathom the former life from which he has come. This demonstrates the transformational power of Jesus Christ. Readers of this book will come face-to-face with a God that does not want to judge them, but wants to redeem them giving them hope and a future.

Don Miller
Superintendent,
Southern Missouri District of the Assemblies of God

As John's brother, I can testify firsthand of the transforming power of God's grace in his life. I encourage you to read his new book, *My Prison Became a Palace*, and share it with everyone you know. I believe God has uniquely gifted and anointed John to lead a generation out of darkness into God's marvelous light.

Brian Alarid
President, America Prays
Founding Pastor, Passion Church

My Prison Became a Palace

My Prison Became a Palace

MY STORY

BY JOHN CALEB ALARID

"My prison became a palace. My dungeon was filled with light. I felt what were like waves of electric liquid love flowing over me for five months."

Cover Design by Hannah-Rose Alarid

ISBN-13: 978-0-7361-0612-2

www.johnalarid.com
www.freedomcitychurch.org

P.O. Box 7001
Springfield, MO 65801

Publishing assistance provided by:
Life Publishers International
1625 North Robberson Avenue
Springfield, Missouri 65803

*Dedicated to my King Jesus, my loving wife, Hannah-Rose,
and our precious daughter, Brooklyn.*

Acknowledgements

I am grateful to my loving family who, in the depth of my addiction and madness, stood by me. Their steadfast faith in Jesus was a lighthouse for this weary traveler sinking in the storms of life. My father, Bob Alarid, brother, Brian (who is now one of my closest friends and advisors), and mother, Carla Heinecke, never wavered. I am grateful also for the ministry of Sonny Arguinzoni of Victory Outreach. It was there that I found freedom in Christ. My first pastor, Tony Garcia of Victory Outreach in Phoenix, was a great positive influence. My mentors and overseers, Dr. Michael Jaffe and Dr. Mark Hausfeld, guided me through Bible school and seminary.

This work would not have been possible without the efforts of Allan Thompson, who edited and formatted the book. He and Dewey Huston were the first ones I went into local jails with while still in Bible school. Many thanks to the most amazing congregation around—Freedom City Church.

As for the eighteen friends I lost to addiction, I try to live my life so that more don't have to die early.

Contents

Foreword

John and I first met in Chicago, when I was teaching an off-site urban missions seminary class he and his lovely wife Hannah were taking. At the same time I was President of the Assemblies of God Theological Seminary in Springfield, Missouri, where the Alarids also lived and worked.

While in Chicago, John asked me what I thought about his starting a church back in Springfield—an Ozark mountain plateau city that is already church-laden, and lacks urban context. Most residents would probably agree that Springfield doesn't need another church, but the Holy Spirit differed with that assumption. Thankfully, John did too, by the same Spirit's leading.

He and Hannah, with a committed core of other visionaries who like-heartedly championed the mission of God in their foresights, prayed, sought counsel and agreed that they would plant Freedom City Church in Springfield.

They secured a location and set a start date for the church, but the location fell through. John approached me about the possibility of using the seminary's William J. Seymour Chapel as a temporary facility where Freedom City Church's fledgling congregation might be able to meet. I pondered his request and thought, "Why not?" The word *seminary* is a Latin derivative that in English means *seedbed*. What better place for a new church to be planted than in our seminary's chapel?

Freedom City Church began and grew quickly. On weekends the seminary foyer (our "Great Hall") was filled with men and women from the streets, because John and others put feet to Springfield's city pavement and proclaimed God's Good News in an area that many would consider too dangerous, or cross-culturally out of reach. On those streets, and thus in seminary, people in dire spiritual, emotional, mental and physical pain have received and accepted the message of the Gospel of Jesus Christ!

One Sunday morning, when I was to preach for Freedom City Church, I marveled that the seminary chapel was filled with the fruit of AGTS's mission, which in simplified terms means reaching lost souls with the Gospel of Jesus. Following the church service that morning, twelve women and men publicly proclaimed their new life in Christ by being water-baptized—in a temporary baptismal tank on the seminary's front lawn, along one of Springfield's busiest streets. As these new disciples of Christ were immersed into and then raised from the water, people driving past the seminary celebrated with us by blowing their horns and giving thumbs up!

Now Freedom City Church has their own facility. The vision and mission to transform lives by the truth of the Bible and the power of the Holy Spirit continue, unabated. It is a wonderful work of God, where His compassion and redemption blow through the hearts and hands of workers who incessantly serve the needs of spiritually and physically broken people.

In connection with Freedom City Church, John and Hannah have also opened the city's first "Hope Homes," residential rehabilitation centers that embody God's mission to help men and women who have life controlling problems be made completely whole.

In *My Prison Became a Palace,* you will be privileged to read a compelling and redemptive narrative, likened in some ways to the transformation of Saul which we read about in the Scriptures.

Absorb every page of John's story. Prepare to be wooed by its witness of God's relentless mercy and grace. Prepare to be challenged and strengthened by its powerful testimony. Finally, allow it to affirm you as you yield your life to the will of God, in whom you can always trust.

Dr. Mark Hausfeld
Professor of Urban and Islamic Studies,
Assemblies of God Theological Seminary
Overseer to the Pastor, Freedom City Church (Springfield, MO)

Introduction

In the world, many people don't believe in God, or they might believe in Him, but don't believe He is active in their lives. I once felt the same way. However, as I now look back over my life, my eyes have been opened by God, and I see that He has been with me every step of the way.

If we don't understand what God is doing, it's because we can't see Him working. He remains hidden, and yet He continues to orchestrate events around us. A prime example of this is in Esther, a book in the Old Testament of the Bible. God is not mentioned in Esther, but through many "coincidences" and turns of events, we see God at work bringing salvation to His people in a hostile environment. In my life, there have been many times when God reached into space and time to help me at the most critical moments. He does that for me, and He is doing that for you, too.

My name is John Caleb Alarid, and I never expected to live to the age of thirty. All around me friends were dying while I was still alive. I didn't understand this—why would God spare *me*?

In another book of the Bible, it says, "But God does not take away life; instead he devises ways so that a banished person may not remain estranged from him" (2 Samuel 14:14). Sin separates us all from God, but through the sacrifice of his Son, Jesus, He restores the banished through faith.

There's a profound quote by author C. S. Lewis that says, "Pain is God's megaphone." Lewis also wrote that

- God is not committed to our comfort here and now. He is committed to our perfection (to be like Jesus) "then and there," that is, over our entire lives.

- God loves us, but he is not going to stop the ache because He can—He is working to accomplish greater things. He is tender, but comfort won't be given if his purpose in trying to deepen our commitment to love others is thwarted.

The Bible teaches us about a great king, David. King David spent many of his years writing prayers to God, which make up most of the Psalms. In one of those prayers, David wrote, "It is good for me that I was afflicted, that I might learn your statutes" (Psalm 119:71).

This book is the story of my journey so far and how God has carried me all the way. It's my prayer that as you read it, you will grow to realize how much God cares for you and how He has carried you in all the circumstances of your journey as well.

He will use your sufferings to grow you and make you more like Christ every day. He uses your "afflictions" to bring light into the darkness of others who find themselves trapped in the same circumstances. They feel hopeless, but you can, and will, bring them the hope only found in the Lord Jesus Christ. Then, look to what the Apostle Paul wrote in Romans 8:18, "For I consider that the sufferings of this present time are not worth comparing with the glory that is to be revealed to us." Be encouraged that God is with you in every step of your life just as He is in mine. We who are His children will be filled with God's joy, peace, and love for eternity.

Chapter 1

CENTRAL AMERICA TO NMMI

I still remember when my parents taught me to walk. We lived in a little house in Costa Rica. Fruit trees surrounded us. As a child, I didn't know what my parents were doing. From my perspective, the two people I loved most stood in front of me, then pulled away so I would go to them. But, when I finally reached them, they would pull away again. This confused me. When I fell, they would smile and pick me up, then again pull away. It made no sense that they would smile when I fell, and then continue to pull away.

This process didn't feel good to me, but through it I learned to walk. Our parents can show us and encourage us how to walk, but ultimately we must do the walking. With God, it is often the same process. He will guide us and encourage us, but at the end of the day we must get up and walk to Him and learn to walk *with* Him. God will pull away at times, so that we can learn how to walk on our own, and it's during those times that we must learn to seek Him and find Him with all our hearts. We must develop our faith. "Without faith it is impossible to please him [God], for whoever would draw near to God must believe that he exists and that he rewards those who seek him" (Hebrews 11:6).

My father taught at a Bible college in Costa Rica in order to pay off his student loans. This was the 1970s. I remember the fruit trees in the yard and spending time riding horses. I also remember falling out of my bed sometimes; too many times for my comfort. So, one night I prayed and asked God to not let me fall off the bed. Several nights later I woke up again as my small body slammed against the floor.

I ran into my parents' bedroom and demanded an answer to my question, "Why did God let me fall out of my bed?" They looked at each other, speechless. With a toddler's imagination, I answered my own question. "Oh, I know! He was sleeping, too!" This satisfied me and I returned to my bed and fell back asleep.

Have you ever asked yourself why God lets you fall?

I have always been a kind of loner and rebel. My natural instinct is to do things my own way. As you continue reading, you'll see this has been the source of much pain throughout my life. One day, as my parents spent time shopping in San José, the capital city of Costa Rica, I followed a dog down the street and got lost. When my parents realized I wasn't with them, they feared the worst; however, they also prayed for the best. After thirty minutes, they walked into the local police station and found me laughing and playing with the chief.

Another time, I took off on my tricycle down the road in front of our house. I just kept on going. I remember seeing familiar sights along the way and thought nothing of it. I couldn't turn around because of the traffic, so I just kept going. Again, my panic-stricken parents noticed my absence and scrambled search parties to find me. Several hours later they found me riding my little red tricycle a mile down the road. I had crossed a major highway and just kept on going.

Have you ever asked yourself why God lets us get lost?

There will always come times when we find ourselves falling down. Sometimes we find ourselves lost. God can use these circumstances to build us up, and He can also help us overcome them.

Disneyland

My mother is originally from San Diego, and we came back to the United States so my parents could travel around and raise money for their work in Latin America. Her family still lives on the West Coast, and they are descendants of German immigrants who arrived in the U.S. in the late 1800s. My father grew up in Monterrey, Mexico. His family is from the New Mexico area, where they have resided for more than five hundred years. They are the offspring of Spanish immigrants and Native Americans (Mestizo / Chicanos).

My forefather, Juan Bautista Alarid, was the last Mexican governor of the land now called New Mexico when it was turned over to the United States in the mid-1800s. At that time, the grant given to my family was revoked, and we lost our land. Juan was offered a position in Mexico City, and most of the Mexican politicians fled south after the United States took over. However, Juan stayed to fight for the rights of his people who were being taken advantage of because they did not speak English. "Grandpa" Juan is considered a hero to many (this writer included). My father's side of the family, including the Alarid, Sanchez, and Campos clans, still live throughout the southwestern United States and in Mexico.

When I was a kid we would often travel to Albuquerque, New Mexico, to spend time with family members in the South Valley area. My great uncle Ben Vigil owned a roofing company there. My younger brother Brian and I loved to go because Ben would let us ride his horses and ATVs. We would ride them all over the labyrinth of little trails around the arroyos in the South Valley. It was always a great time. I would spend summers there with my great grandmother, Anita Sanchez, who spoke Spanish and broken English with a thick accent. Even when I was strung out on drugs and in and out of jail, my great-grandmother would stick up for me. She would say, *"No es mala gente, tiene problemitas pero no es mala gente,"* (He is not a bad person; he just has some bad habits).

My *abuelita* (great-grandma) lived on 67th Street and Central on the west side of Albuquerque. When her house was built, it was farther west than any other house at the time. Back then only a dirt road led out that way. My great-grandfather, Senor Sanchez, was a bartender, although the family said he never drank. He died when I was young and I have no memories of him. My *abuelita* Sanchez was the funniest woman I ever met, although I don't think she did it intentionally. She always laughed and joked. I remember that she was nearly blind in both eyes and only her peripheral vision worked. She would watch her *telenovelas* (Spanish soap operas) with her head about an inch from the screen, but her head was turned so it looked like she was watching the television with her ear. She was nearly deaf too, so the old television was always turned up full blast. Her soap operas could easily be heard from the front yard.

As time went on, her once keen memory worsened. She would always say, "Oh, I forgot to remember" in a thick Hispanic accent. She was a devout Catholic, with her rosary beads and pictures of Christ and the Virgin all over her house. Invariably, as anyone was leaving her home she would come to the front window and do the sign of the cross over the loved ones as they went. I miss her greatly.

When I was four, my family was in California at the headquarters of the missionary organization they were affiliated with. We went to Disneyland for a day, and while walking around I spotted an old-fashioned shooting gallery that looked like a saloon. You would put in your money and then fire the rifles at different targets, knocking over bottles, chairs, and dishes in the little Wild West saloon. A light would come out of the rifle and the idea was to hit the little red targets, like a big video game. It was the best part of Disneyland. I played a few times and then my parents were ready to move on, but I wanted to continue playing. Being a stubborn kid, I just stayed there.

My parents said they were going to leave me if I did not come. Normally this would work, but I was determined to shoot some more things. So I stayed, although I did not have any money. I figured I would call their bluff. But they did leave me and went to Tom Sawyer Island, while I remained on the stool at the shooting gallery. I soon realized that without money you could not shoot anything because no light came out of the rifle.

I quickly lost interest and walked to a little grassy area with a tree across from the shooting gallery to wait on my parents. As I stood there, I felt the presence of God, but I don't know if I would have described it that way. I knew it was a powerful presence of a sacred being, although I could not see anyone. At any rate, I prayed and asked Jesus to come into my heart. I heard this prayer before when my father spoke on his missionary journeys, but this time my prayer was personal. I still remember that day as if it were yesterday. Many years later I would stand at a shooting gallery on Santa Monica Pier and hear God say, "Do you remember when we first met?"

Later that night, as we were getting ready for bed at my aunt's home, I decided to tell my parents about my prayer. I walked into their room and said, "I asked Jesus into my heart." They responded, "Okay John, now go to bed." I stood there in shock. They didn't seem to care about the most important day of my life. I stood there and began crying and said, "It's for real, Dad."

My parents finally realized how serious a moment this was. My father called me over onto the bed and began to talk to me about my experience. I told him that when they were at Tom Sawyer Island I asked the Lord to come into my life. Years later my father told me in a joking way that at the time he wondered how God could meet such a little rebel, since I had refused to obey my parents and remained at that shooting gallery.

Do you ever ask yourself that? *How can God meet the rebel in me?* For me, personally, I never forgot that experience. It is the most vivid memory of my childhood. However, as I grew older, I came to believe it was just the delusion of a child, or possibly was brought about by the need to fit into my Christian environment. At any rate, at four years of age I asked the God of the universe to come into my life, and He did. Forty years later I sit here writing this story and I can say that although I left God and rebelled against Him, He never left me.

When I was six, my parents and my brother and I were visiting Lakewood Church in Houston, Texas. Their pastor, John Osteen, supported my parents financially from time to time. We were near the front row this night. I remember the elevated stage with a series of steps to take in order to reach the top. It had the shape of a half moon. We attended every service when my parents were in from the missionary field and much of my childhood was spent in church services, most of the time asleep under the front pew.

However, this night was different. The speaking caught my attention. I do not know why. As John Osteen preached like a house on fire, I sensed the presence of God and a thought, like a voice that did not originate with me, said, "One day you are going to do this." This thought ran through my mind the remainder of the service. The presence of God electrified the entire atmosphere. After the Disneyland experience, and that of learning to walk in Costa Rica, this is the third most vivid memory of my younger years.

To me, this stage of my life is characterized by the faithfulness of God. In 2 Timothy 2:13, the apostle Paul wrote, "If we are faithless, he remains faithful—for he cannot deny himself." The nature of God is to be faithful. He cannot contradict His character. His loving-kindness and faithfulness leads us to repentance.

The Spirit of God wonderfully moved on me as a child. It is God's will that *all* be saved. Again, it is God's will that all be saved—and this includes you, even if you don't believe it. This God of love, compassion, and grace does not wish the death of even one sinner. Humanity is broken and in need of a savior. We need the grace of God to live pure lives. I am more certain now than I was during the worst years of my addiction that in me dwells no good thing, except Christ. I believe that each one of us, when we are honest, will admit that we are aware of our depravity. Along with Paul, we find that the things we want to do, we do not do, and the things we do not want to do, we do (Romans 7). There is something inside us pushing to do things we know are contrary to our moral law and standards. In spite of our condition, God reaches down to draw us to Himself. How could a holy and good God want anything to do with me? Oh the wondrous mystery of the goodness of God! "While we were still sinners, Christ died for us" (Romans 5:8). The righteous died for the unrighteous. He took the punishment that we deserve.

We stand before God based on the sacrifice of Christ. These Christian tenets and biblical truths make sense after we have a personal encounter with God. An encounter with God changes everything, and it's something we need more than anything else.

When I was in third grade we moved to Houston, Texas from Latin America. I remember getting into a fight with one of the neighborhood kids (I was constantly in fist fights). The kid's father came out and started pushing me. My mom came out of the house and said to the father, *"Dejaolo. Vete!"* (Leave him alone! Get out of here!). He looked at her and said, "Go back to Mexico you **** spick lover." His words carried such contempt and hatred. That hurt me because I grew up around my father's side of the family. This was my first experience with racism.

We left Houston when an uncle was arrested on suspicion of organized crime activity, and the story was broadcast on the evening news. As a kid, I remember admiring my uncles that had big homes and fancy cars. Later in life I would follow in their footsteps of lucrative criminal activity.

New Mexico Military Institute (NMMI)

My parents divorced for a couple of years during the time of my uncle's arrest. My brother and I went to live with our father in Monterrey, Mexico, where I attended eighth and ninth grades, or *primera de secundaria* as they call it in Mexico. We then returned to Albuquerque, where I did not get along with my father. I was already a very rebellious teenager and wanted to do my own thing. In 1988, I decided to move to where my mother lived in Dayton, Tennessee, where she was taking classes at Bryan University. I attended the local high school for a few months and even endured pre-season football practices. Before the end of the year, my father and mother decided to get remarried, and the whole family moved to Sterling Heights, Michigan, a Detroit suburb.

In Michigan, I was kicked out of one school for arguing with a teacher. I began skipping school to go hang out with friends and smoke marijuana. Once again, I was kicked out of school for disrespecting a teacher. At the next high school, I missed over one month of classes before a school administrator finally called my parents. A few days later I got arrested for shoplifting at a local department store where my mother worked. The school made a deal with me that if I came back, I would not have to make up the work. I could just pick up with the rest of the class. I did complete the tenth grade.

On my sixteenth birthday, I came home so drunk that my friends had to carry me to the door and hand me over to my parents. I told them I was not feeling well and someone gave me what I thought was an aspirin and now I felt sick. My mom believed me. My father came up to my room and told me I needed to go puke up the alcohol and that it would make me feel better. "What?" I exclaimed with a contrived look of shock on my face. "You heard me," my father said. He obviously did not buy the aspirin story. I did as he told me and proceeded to the bathroom where I spent the next half an hour puking. He was right. I felt much better.

During this time, I had a fake ID from Mexico that said I was over 21. I was the "big man" who provided alcohol for all my friends. I had a part time job at Hardees, and some of us employees had a hustle going which would bring us each an extra forty to sixty dollars a night. I worked as the drive-through attendant while a friend cooked. We would just add up the customers' food on the register and then zero it out. When they came to the window to pay I would give them their change from a cup next to the register. My life was going nowhere fast.

My parents sent me to New Mexico Military Institute (NMMI) in Roswell for my junior year. We have had many relatives graduate from this reputable institution. It is an academy and college prep school.

Unfortunately, my parents separated again shortly thereafter and were divorced again after that.

I moved into my new home in Echo troop at NMMI in August, 1989. I was seventeen, a little old for my class because I had been held back in the third grade when my family moved to the states from Central America.

At NMMI, the new cadets are called RATs (Recruit-at-Training) and have zero privileges. We had to march in the gutter next to the sidewalk everywhere we went. When we came out of our rooms we had to stand at attention and say, "Cadet Alarid, JC, requests permission to rest." Then one of the seniors would say, "Rest," and we could move to our destination without looking right or left.

Each night we had mandatory study hall from six to ten p.m. We had to be at our desks on time. Staff would walk around and check on us. If we were not in our place, we would be written up.

This environment worked very well for me. I learned how to study, and I held a 4.0 average. This didn't keep me out of trouble, however. I still had my fake ID. I would rent hotel rooms on weekends and pick up some beer so we could get drunk. We were required to wear our uniforms everywhere we went, but we would be easily spotted if we had them on. So, the room was also a great place to change into our street clothes.

One time we drank a few beers and put the rest on ice. Three or four of us went for a walk around Roswell. After our short excursion, I decided to head back to the hotel. The police soon knocked at the door. They asked if I had rented the room, and I said, "Yes." They said management had called them because they saw cadets with beer. They asked if I went to NMMI. I assured them that I did not. They then noticed all the uniforms hanging over chairs in the room. I told them those belonged to some of my friends. The problem with that lie was that all our uniforms had name tags, so the officers took the uniforms. I tried to pull my nametag off quickly, but it was too late.

The officers said they were going to take the uniforms and turn them over to the NMMI police. My heart sank. I knew I was busted. After they left, the other cadets returned and we headed back to campus where we had to sneak into our rooms. We felt like commandos, using our very limited training to get back to our rooms without being detected by the staff. We made it, but several hours later we were called down to the guard shack where our urine was tested for alcohol. Needless to say, we all failed. Our uniforms were returned to us as the staff laughed and mocked us by saying, "Next time don't leave your name tags on." I received one hundred "tours" for this infraction. One tour is equivalent to marching for one hour around the squares in the middle of the barracks area. They were to be done on weekends so as not to interfere with studies. I spent Saturdays and Sundays marching around in circles for the rest of my first semester.

When Christmas break came I spent two weeks marching around in circles eight hours a day until I finished. Everyone else went home and I remained marching in the snow. It was a very lonely experience. Finally I finished, and my dad arrived to pick me up to celebrate Christmas. I felt bad because I had let him down.

One of my best friends and fellow RATs was a Muslim guy from Michigan, named Shakir. His family was originally from Bangladesh. He had a prayer rug that he would pull out to pray several times a day, and many guys would harass him for his beliefs. After ninety days we were allowed to get school-color blankets to put on our walls. We could pin up pictures of family or whatever we wanted on them. Well, most of us wanted to put up pictures of women in bathing suits. The *Sports Illustrated* swimsuit issue was a favorite. Shakir refused to join in, saying, "I can't have half-naked women on my wall because I have to pray in here." Everyone laughed at him about this, but it pierced my heart. He believed in and took a stand for his faith. At this time, I stood far from God. The God I had known as a child felt a million miles away, if He existed at all. Then I saw this Muslim guy being more devout and bold than any so-called Christians my age.

From that day forward I had a renewed respect for Shakir. We became very close. I often joked with him about his faith, but inside I wished I had the courage to take a stand for something I believed in. I also began to wonder about the belief that Christianity was the only true faith. If so, was Shakir fooled? He was raised as a Muslim and it was part of his culture, so surely it must be real. This began my belief in relative truth. I believed that since he believed it was true, it was true for him. Likewise, since my parents believed in their Christian religion and God, it was true for them. I believed that we could all believe what we wanted and as long as we were sincere and true to ourselves, our version of reality was actual reality. This also worked as a salve for my conscience as I could now do all the things that I was taught not to do with impunity. I could do my own thing and ride my little red tricycle wherever I wanted.

I came back and finished the school year with a 4.0 average. I also took my ACT with a score of 27. The following year the school celebrated its one-hundred-year anniversary. Now I was an upperclassman, responsible for training the new RATs. However, I did not haze, nor did I talk down to the new guys as most others did. I felt like it was an abuse of power. As long as they did what they were supposed to do, I left them alone. Shakir and I planned on attending the Air Force Academy in Colorado Springs. The superintendent of NMMI, General Stewart, was the former superintendent of the Air Force Academy. Shakir and I were selected to be NMMI class officers and our future looked bright.

However, close to the end of the first semester of our senior year, we ran into some trouble. There was an ongoing feud between the students at NMMI and the local high school students at Roswell-Goddard High School and Roswell High School. One day, as I drove to the bank with Shakir and another friend, Dan, we noticed some local boys in a car glaring at us. We had our uniforms on so they knew who we were. We proceeded to exchange words and they took off.

Later that day, as we pulled down the street behind NMMI, we noticed some guys hanging out on the porch of a house with what appeared to be a keg of beer. They signaled for us to turn into the driveway, so we did, assuming we might be able to drink some beer and maybe meet some local girls. When we pulled in I recognized one of the guys as the driver of the vehicle we had an altercation with earlier. More guys came out of the house and there were about twenty-five of them around my Monte Carlo. The guy said, "Get out of the car." I said, "No, thanks." Then they completely surrounded my car. It looked bleak for us. My friend Dan had left his pistol under the front seat, as we had gone out shooting earlier. Shakir, who sat in the passenger seat, pulled out the pistol and pointed at the guy at my window. He said, "They got a gun." That made them all back away from the vehicle and we pulled out and went back to campus. Later that night we decided to head across the street and settle the score with those guys. A party was going on and the house was jammed with high school kids.

About 10:00 p.m., someone yelled, "toot fight!" The locals had called the cadets "toots" for many decades. Eventually the cadets adopted the name. A "toot fight" was the call to come and help your brothers. The cadets were very close, like brothers who fought among themselves, but turned on anyone else who tried to start something. We all would band together and any attackers would have to deal with the whole group. About twenty of us left to go across the street, but by the time we got there it was more like sixty. One guy even had the color guard pole with the troop name on the flag. It must have looked intimidating to the guys at the party. As we crossed the street "retreat" began to play over the loudspeaker. The song played every night at the same time. Anyone outside when it played would have to stand at attention until it finished.

So there we were, about to go get rowdy with those guys, and as the mob crossed the street "retreat" started over the loudspeaker. Comically, we all stopped and stood at attention until it ended. Then we started to yell at the high school guys, Before a fight started, the NMMI police showed up and stopped us. We were told to go back to campus and we did. Two hours later they came to my room and asked if they could search my vehicle. They searched and found the handgun under the front seat and a shotgun in the trunk.

We were written up, and it took several weeks and an investigation, but all three of us were eventually suspended. Shakir and I were leaders at the top of our class. We were academy prep students on our way to the Air Force Academy. Dan was the son of a prominent attorney in Albuquerque. His dad was an alumnus and had attended NMMI with the current commandant of cadets. This was a serious issue since we were not supposed to have firearms on campus. Also, the owner of the house where we had the altercation was an employee of NMMI. The kid's mom was a barber at the school. We were all suspended for one semester. Shakir and I were told by the superintendent that he regretted this decision because he did not want our careers to be hindered because of one mistake in high school (which NMMI really was). He promised if we came back after our semester of suspension, he would write a personal recommendation to the Air Force Academy and guarantee we would get in.

With a heavy heart, I called my dad to tell him I had been suspended. My dad and grandfather had come to see me often, and I could tell that they were very proud of me. They even treated me like a man worthy of respect. My dad just remained silent on the other end when I told him the news. I could hear him crying through the phone, and then he said, "Why do you keep doing this to me?" My heart broke. I had no answer. I apologized.

My father had wanted to attend West Point and was even accepted, but he met my mother in Bible school, got married, and I was born less than a year later.

Shakir and I drove back to Albuquerque and I dropped him off at the airport, and then went to my father's house. My father enrolled me in Menaul School in Albuquerque. Many members of the Campos side of my family had graduated from this school. Shakir enrolled back at NMMI the next semester and went on to graduate from the Air Force Academy.

Chapter 2

From Menaul to Stupid

For several months, I spent my time feeling as though once again I had blown it. I missed NMMI, even the early wake ups and inspections. Most of all I missed my friends. When you live with people, it seems like you either end up hating each other or loving each other. I made some great friends at the military school—Ty, Tristan, Shakir, and Dan, to name a few. So, I went to Menaul School and attended honors classes. My last semester I pulled a 4.1 GPA. Shakir had come back into town on his way to NMMI and tried to convince me to go, too. We were guaranteed to get into the Air Force Academy. I declined. I had met a girl at Menaul and we believed we were the most in love couple that ever lived on the planet. My father did not approve. He had hopes of me going back to NMMI and on to the AFA.

I moved out of my dad's home during the second semester of my senior year and moved into my dad's brother's house. Uncle Ronny owned a pest control company and had recently divorced, so it was just us two bachelors in the house. He gave me a job and even let my girlfriend stay the night whenever she wanted. My girlfriend, Michelle, drove a brand new white Corvette convertible. I left my Monte Carlo at my dad's when I moved out because he had bought it. This was a very hard time in my life. I thought my dad was being unreasonable about my girlfriend, and I felt like he was still mad at me for getting kicked out of NMMI. The truth is, he just wanted the best for me, but I was almost a high school graduate and thought I knew more than anybody. I drove the Corvette home after dropping Michelle off at her house on school nights since I had no car and lived on the other side of town. I was accepted into the University of New Mexico with a full ride NM Scholars Scholarship for my 3.85 cumulative average and 27 ACT score.

In fact my high school counselor said, "You could get into any school you want. Are you sure you want to go to UNM?" I was sure. I was in love. I moved in with my high school sweetheart shortly after graduation. Her father actually paid for our apartment, and I worked for my uncle's company, Bug Busters, to pay the rent, and to have money for alcohol and marijuana, of course.

University of New Mexico

After my senior year in high school, I went by my middle name, Caleb. The South-siders, my gang, called me *Coyote*. A coyote is half wolf and half dog. I was half Hispanic on my father's side and half Norwegian on my mother's. I flowed in different scenes quite easily. I felt at home in the hood, a college classroom, or even an exclusive restaurant. I lived as a chameleon of sorts. This was an advantage to me in the dope game. Everyone felt as though I was one of them, but I felt like I was just a big phony.

UNM is a school of more than twenty thousand students. The Grateful Dead (the band) ranked it the best college to attend along with the University of California at Santa Cruz. Drugs were rampant. My first semester I met a guy named Pedro. (Pedro has now been in a Nevada prison since 1999). Pedro came from the west side of Albuquerque. My family is mostly from the South Valley, but we hit it off. We met in Spanish class. We both spoke Spanish but more of a street Chicano Spanish. Both of our families were native New Mexicans, therefore, we were the local boys. Many students were from out of state. Through family connections and being fluent in Spanish, I would later get lined up with a major Mexican drug cartel.

My girlfriend and I ended up having problems, and I moved out during my first semester in college. I moved into an apartment at Oak Tree Park Apartments with our neighbor, George. He had graduated from the University of Texas at Austin and had moved to Albuquerque after his mother died the year before. They were very close and it was too hard for him to remain in Austin. We got along great at first, but eventually he got sick of my all-night parties. During this time, my friend from NMMI, Tristan, another local Albuquerque guy, moved in to stay on the couch. To this day, I remember him as one of my best friends, although we've lost touch and I have not spoken to him for years.

Tristan had seen me go into cocaine induced seizures many times. He also saw me go from a 4.0 high school student to a hopeless junkie in a very short time. Years later, when Tristan graduated from the University of Texas at Austin, he called my dad's house and asked, "Is John still alive?" My dad told him that I was alive and doing better.

I began to use more and more drugs. I smoked pot daily and dropped liquid LSD 25. I bought sheets of acid, pounds of pot, and supplied many UNM students with drugs. My friend Mike H. lived in the dorms where hundreds of students were always looking for drugs. I soon realized how much money could be earned at the dorms because I could get the drugs in bulk very cheaply—simple economics.

One time while on acid I was driving east on a one way street, where if you drove the speed limit you could hit all the lights green. I figured if I doubled the speed limit I would hit all the lights green as well. This makes sense while under the influence of LSD. I made it past a few green lights at one hundred miles per hour, but then a light turned red. For some reason, I thought I could keep going and go right through the other cars. Like the guy from the *Terminator* movie, I could just melt right to the other side. I almost gave it a try, but then stopped. Had I been just a little more out of it, I would have kept going and would most likely not be here today.

Tristan and I would trip for days on end. We would take a few hits the first day and double or triple them and continue going for days. During this time my thoughts changed. I don't know how to explain it, but my worldview drastically shifted. One night at Oak Tree Park, Tristan and I got a gallon of Tequila Gold. We started drinking at about 11:00 a.m. We played quarter for several hours and drank like fish. We drank just to get drunk. I never was a social drinker or a social drug user. I am an all or nothing type person. Like wanting to always do things my own way, this has been the source of much pain in my life.

Later that night, completely inebriated, I went into my room and started talking to God. I said, "God, you have made yourself real to my father and mother. Some people talk as if they have met you. If you will show up and talk to me, I will believe in you. If not, I am going to go my own way. It is up to you." I gave God an ultimatum. Surely if He was God, and He loved me, He would meet my demand. I must admit a part of me feared God would actually show up and then I would have to give up all the fun I was having. But, God did not show up. I heard and saw nothing. In fact, I had never felt more alone than I did then. After several minutes of silence, I began to beat the wall with my fists shouting, "Show yourself to me!" I guess I beat it for a long while because blood flowed from my knuckles. God didn't show up. I was definitely free to live life my own way.

Like the Israelites in the Old Testament book of Judges, I went on to do whatever was right *in my own eyes*. The Israelites, who fell into shocking depravity, did so because they were the generation after Moses and Joshua. They had not been at the foot of Mt. Sinai when God came down, nor had they seen the Red Sea parted. They said, "If God is God, where are all the wonders that our forefathers told us about?"

God does not have grandchildren, only children. We cannot live on the faith of our parents or a former generation. Being a Christ-follower is about having a personal encounter with Jesus. It is an intimate relationship more real and satisfying than any other on this planet. Somehow, I sensed this in my heart but had yet to experience it. After that night, I did in fact go my own way. My demands were not met, so I assumed that God must not care about me. Several months later I mentioned to my mom that I had asked God to reveal himself to me, but He did not. She said, "I am so glad you prayed that because that is a prayer that God will answer." At the time, I didn't realize how right she was.

After my apartment lease ended, I moved to a house several blocks from the school. Tristan went with me. Pete, an acquaintance, introduced me to a friend of his named Alex Stowell. Alex was a big white boy from Los Angeles and was a fullback for the University of New Mexico Lobos football team. We instantly liked each other. At that time, I was moving a lot of marijuana and acid. Another friend of ours was Eric (Big-E), an African-American guy from Los Angeles who had also played football for the Lobos.

Alex and Big-E were bringing in about seven kilos a month from California and cooking up rock (crack or freebase cocaine). I saw that there was money in it, so I began picking up ounces of cocaine from my drug friends in the South Valley. Eventually, through family connections and because I speak Spanish, I became involved with a major Mexican cartel.

At nineteen years old I was buying about a kilo of cocaine and five to ten pounds of weed a week. I sold crack to street dealers.

A rock usually costs twenty dollars, but a *dub* is double up, two for twenty dollars. We would sell ten for a *c note* (one hundred dollars). There was a lot of money in purchasing weight and selling in small quantities, but there was a greater risk because of the number of people that one would have to deal with. More people equals greater chance of getting busted; however, at the time, I thought I was invincible.

Initially, I sold only powder cocaine to college students, athletes, and people at the bar scene. I was very careless in the early days before I got busted. I would go to downtown bars with a bag of papers (a paper is twenty dollars' worth in a paper *foldy*) and sell to many people. I loved being the guy with the dope. I had my entourage with me and I would buy drinks for everyone all night. They would make deals for me all night. When we came to a bar we were quickly escorted to the front of the line and given the best seats in the bar.

I would make so much money that it did not fit in my pockets. I would have to go to the car to drop off money and pick up more papers. Most of the bouncers were UNM football players and they knew I dealt drugs. At many places, the drinks were free. I began using more cocaine. I remember wondering, "Will I ever get addicted to this stuff like they say?" I thought I would be fine. I was just having fun and making lots of money. I was not like the *clucks*, slang for the crack heads that came to buy rock with their teeth missing, looking like bums, and their kids in rickety old strollers. There were also plenty of them looking for a *front* (to advance someone drugs for cash). These people were the scum of the earth. I was driving a brand new red sports car and my clothes were at the height of fashion. I was making more than a thousand dollars per day. Big deals went down once or twice a week, and I would make thousands of dollars for a few minutes of work. I was on top of the world.

Gangsta rap was very popular at the time. N.W.A., Too Short, Tupac, Snoop Dogg, Dr. Dre, and others were all rapping about the life we were actually living. Other people were the ones who used needles. They were very sketchy people. I was sure I was better than those dregs of humanity. I was not an addict. I was a pusher. I was just the supplier who liked to party a little. I quickly gained respect on the street. The homies from the South Valley looked up to me.

Everywhere I went people were overly nice to me and very respectful. I was invited to all the parties: Frat parties; Lobos football parties; the bar scene after parties; and gang parties. I was quite popular. It felt like I was in a movie. I was watching this character that looked like me on a screen. It did not seem to be real life. This was the early '90s and pagers were the thing. Everyone had his or her own code so I knew who was calling. Then, after their code, they would plug in how much money they wanted to spend on whatever drugs they wanted.

I started to move marijuana by the pound or more. It was just too bulky and there was not as much money in selling it in small amounts. These were the glory days of the *game*. I was sending marijuana up the East Coast and to Illinois, Wisconsin, and New York. I was paying my suppliers about two hundred dollars for a pound of marijuana and clients would pay five hundred to eight hundred per pound in town and twice that much up North. Weed went for at least sixty dollars a quarter ounce up North, so the guys pushing there were making a killing. People would buy up to fifty pounds at a time. It was easy money.

I was making more money than college graduates and business owners. I began to think I was too good to attend college. The life I was living brought delusions of grandeur. I began to believe I was this extremely cool and tough guy. I played the part. I got a handgun and began treating people with contempt. I became aloof and very arrogant. I treated everyone as if they worked for me. People would come detail my car for drugs. Girls would clean my house for drugs. I was *the man*. The universe revolved around me.

Then I learned to cook up rock cocaine with baking soda. Alex and Big-E would cook up rock by the kilo in mayonnaise jars. My friend Pedro, who was my right hand man at this time, introduced me to the major players in the dope game and was my bodyguard and collections guy. One day he brought me a glass pipe as a gift. I still remember the day he walked up to my door at my house on Sycamore Street, the one near UNM. He had his backpack in one hand and said, "I have a gift for you." We went inside and he pulled out a glass pipe. It had a bowl with a glass stem coming out of it. I was like, "Cool! I will get some weed to put in it." He laughed at me and said, "It's not for weed Holmes, it's for rock." The crazy thing is, I had cooked up a lot of rock and sold it in my short dope dealing career, but I had only smoked it on top of marijuana as a "white cap." I snorted cocaine all day and sometimes all night, but had not sat down and smoked rock. I thought that was only for the *clucks*.

That afternoon I cooked up a half ounce. Pedro, myself, and a few others sat down to smoke rock out of my new gift. Pete took about a half gram of rock and put in the pipe and handed it to me. He held the lighter for me because there is a technique to smoking crack which I was soon to master. You do not want to just put the flame directly on it. At any rate, he lit it and I took a big hit then held it in like it was a bong hit of marijuana. My ears began to ring like a freight train was coming and my entire body pulsated. I had never felt anything like that. It was much better than snorting lines. Later, I would move on to shooting cocaine intravenously.

We continued to smoke all day. For the next few weeks I smoked rock. I began to get very paranoid and eventually taped up all the windows so that no one could see in or out.

One time there were some people over doing drugs at my house. I was very generous with drugs, but I used that to manipulate people. On that day, I thought I was missing a couple ounces of cocaine from my room. There were probably fifteen people partying at my house, guys and girls. Some were Tristan's friends who only smoked weed and stayed away from the harder stuff. I locked the doors and said, "No one is leaving until I get my two ounces of cocaine back." I brandished my .357 Smith & Wesson and slammed it down on the table. I said, "Someone took my dope! Nobody's leaving. Take off your clothes." I told Pedro to search everybody. I told them it was for their own good to prove their innocence. It was a crazy scene. Everyone was searched and my dope was not there. Later that morning I found the missing ounces stuffed behind one of my dressers. I never told anyone that I found that missing dope.

I had several people that would go around and drop off drugs for me. Tristan worked for me for a time, too. I became increasingly paranoid and arrogant. My old friends became alienated as I began to hang out with a rougher crowd. I was nineteen years old and most of my new friends were older. I started thinking the cops (whom I believed to be the enemy) were watching me. There were times when I would walk outside my house and see cars lined up with people in them. People would come to pick up drugs and leave their friends in the car. I repeatedly told them not to bring anyone I did not know and *never* leave people in the car. I would yell and degrade friends for breaking my rules. I was turning into a monster.

One day we were up for several days smoking rock. We had broken down a big mirror and placed it on the coffee table to make chocolate rocks. Chocolate rocks are made by taking alcohol and rinsing the pipe that is black with resin. You then pour it out on the mirror and light it on fire. The alcohol burns up and what is left is pure free base cocaine.

That night, Steve, a friend of mine from NMMI days, dropped by. He came to the door and could hear people inside, but all the windows were taped so no light could be seen. The window in the door had a cardboard box taped over it, and when someone came a little piece was moved to the side to peek out. My friend was at the door, unaware of how crazy the scene was. I allowed my old military school buddy to come in. What he saw was a living room full of cracked out people with glass pipes and lighters everywhere. There were shotguns and handguns in plain view. On the coffee table was the huge piece of broken mirror. As he came in one of the glass pipes was shaken with alcohol that was then thrown on the mirror and lit until it burned up. The "chocolate rocks" were scraped into a pile by a young lady with eyes big as melons and a faraway gaze.

Then I took a pistol out of my pants and put it on the table next to my chair and offered my friend a seat. Everyone paused for a moment, but when they realized that he was a friend they picked up where they had left off. As the night went on everyone mostly avoided Steve, except for me. A pager went off and I looked at it and handed it to Pedro and asked him to call them back and tell them come to the Circle K convenience store at Central and University and page when they arrived. This was standard operating procedure.

Steve just remained standing and silent throughout. I had known this guy in high school and at one time we were close friends. He was at UNM now. I saw him occasionally on campus and at the bars. The girl that had scraped up the chocolate rocks filled a pipe and handed it to me and then held the fire to the bowl for me. I took a monster hit and then blew the smoke into the girl's mouth directly. She held it in then blew out a mushroom cloud right to where Steve was standing. He was enveloped by a cloud of freebase cocaine smoke. Then Jack, the campus debate champ, took a huge hit while standing by the fireplace. As he exhaled he fell to the ground and appeared to be unconscious. I thought he was dead, but he eventually got up. All this was completely normal for me at that time.

After a while, Steve politely insisted that he had to go. He just wanted to drop by to say "hi." He left abruptly and I did not think anything of it. The next day someone told me that Steve had been at the bars saying, "Stay away from Caleb because I went by his house and they are smoking crack, and selling drugs, and there are guns all over the house. The windows are all taped up, and everyone is paranoid." When I heard this I was enraged. I did not appreciate Steve telling about my business down at the bars. I got his number and called him. I said, "What's up, Steve? I heard you were talking smack at the bars." He had broken the unspoken code of silence. He apologized profusely and said it would not happen again. I did not speak to Steve for a very long time.

I was not cognizant of just how crazy my life had become in such a short time. The only people I had contact with were customers and suppliers. The Albuquerque underworld was my home. I was then only twenty, but I was a major player in the dope scene in Albuquerque. I also sent large amounts up the east coast. Students that attended UNM found they could get drugs from me and make money back home up north and back east.

My friends at college were trying to graduate and do something with their lives. They just wanted to party and maybe make a little spending money along the way. My friends from the neighborhood were much more hardcore than the college students. Their lives revolved around drugs and violence. With the backing of my crew from a Chicano street gang, I knew these college students were no match for me. I had quickly noticed that they were intimidated by me, so I played the part. My group even decided that if people wanted to sell drugs on campus, they had to come through us. We were street people from Albuquerque, so all those rich kids from out of town needed to respect us. *Burque* (what the locals called Albuquerque) was our town. The out-of-towners were on our turf so that's the way it was. It seems almost ludicrous now, but at the time it made complete sense.

I ended up not attending many of my UNM classes because there was just no time for something as trivial as college courses. I was caught up by the drug scene and was not even aware of it. I started getting even more paranoid. My neighbor, Jason, sold drugs for me. He told me several times, "You're getting very skinny, and your house is drawing a lot of attention. You should slow it down a bit." I did not appreciate him getting into my business at the time. Later, I realized he was one of my few true friends.

I *had* noticed that things were getting out of control. I personally sold to more than fifty people a day, not counting supplying other kids who sold dope for me. I was drawing "way too much heat." All it would take is for one of my sellers to get caught and they would probably "snitch" me out.

At times throughout this drug-induced madness, I would have moments of lucidity and ask myself where God had gone. I felt like I was just an actor playing the part of a cool drug dealer, but deep inside I was a scared little boy who just wanted people to like, and maybe even love, him.

As a child, I was insecure around girls. I had been a fat kid until I got the mumps my freshman year in high school. I lost about thirty pounds and the weight just stayed off. Now I had plenty of women interested in me, and even throwing themselves at me. I was too sold on myself to comprehend that they were attracted by the drugs and the money, not me.

Since we moved around a lot when I was growing up, I never had opportunities to build any stability through life-long relationships. I found any "friends and family" in the drug culture. I gradually realized that these people did not care about me. They only cared about themselves. I was just the guy who had the party favors. Even worse, I found out that *I* only cared about myself.

The culture on campus was extremely anti-God and more specifically, anti-Christ. It was cool to be a Buddhist, Muslim, or Atheist, but Christianity was not at all fashionable. The professors spoke openly against Christianity. During this time, the little faith I did have dried up in the desert of intellectualism. How could it be that I just happened to be born into a family that believed the only truth on the planet? What about people who lived in other countries that had not ever heard of Jesus? This did not seem fair to me. An all-powerful and loving God would not condemn people to hell who had never heard of Him would he? What about my friend Shakir, the follower of Islam? Surely, God would honor a man who would not put a picture of a woman in a bathing suit on his dorm room wall because he had to pray in there. He just grew up in a culture that had a different religion, that's all.

However, my parents were adamant believers in Christ and were sincere in their beliefs. They believed as strongly as Shakir did. If there was absolute truth, then one of them was right and the other wrong. How could I reconcile that? That's where the tension lay. I decided to stick with my belief in relative truth. Whatever a person truly believed and followed was that person's reality and truth. Whatever a person wanted to believe and practice was cool as long as that person was sincere. This was a common belief among the people I had always hung out with. Many of my cousins were Catholic, and yet they lived their lives just like anyone who didn't go to church. Most were "nominal" Catholics who attended church on Easter or for a funeral. They sincerely believed that they were saved from hell because they were members of the Catholic church. My father was one of the few Protestants in the family.

This whole God thing was confusing, but somewhere deep inside I knew that God existed, although He chose not to be active in my life. That was one of my many misconceptions about God. A much bigger misconception was my belief in relative truth. In essence, belief in relative truth makes humans into God. I was choosing to follow a god whose likeness I made into what I thought it should be. The god of relative truth bears no resemblance to the God of the Bible. Of course, I had never read the Bible, so how would I know?

The proverbial downward spiral happened to me very quickly between the years of 1991 and 1993. I would do cocaine non-stop until I finally passed out because my body could not take it anymore.

Then I would wake up and start the process all over again. I would go through a fifth a day and many Valium pills to take the edge off the cocaine. I started drinking Jagermeister and ended up on Jack Daniels whiskey. I had bottles piled up from the floor to the ceiling in my house. It was a makeshift altar to the god of hedonism.

My philosophy was, "Eat, drink and be merry, for tomorrow we die." If God was not real then life really had no meaning. We lived only once, so I believed that we should do whatever our hearts desired. I felt that I was a kind of revolutionary. I broke the law like Robin Hood to give people what they wanted. Who was the government to tell people they could not use street drugs, and then allow pharmaceutical companies to sell drugs that had the same effect? Those companies made billions of dollars each year and had one of the most powerful lobbies in Washington. It was all about money and control, but I was not part of that. After all, I rationalized, I was not hurting anyone. I only sold to adults who had the right to do a little dope if they wanted.

I stopped going to any classes at all. I would leave my house because of paranoia, and go stay in hotels because I thought the cops were going to bust in at any time. Then at the hotels I would get paranoid and move to other hotels the same night. I sold cocaine to more and more people without really even knowing them. We sold a lot of rock. We sold in the student ghetto, the war zone, the sticks, and the Kirk, neighborhoods in Albuquerque. We (my crew, Big E, and Alex) had opened up several crack houses around the area. Alex and I would hang out a lot. He was the only person I could relate to because he was in the game, too. I looked at all other people outside my group as *clucks* that just wanted to get drugs from me. This was not always the truth, but it was my delusional perception.

Alex and I would go to bars and parties and throw money and drugs around like we were "shot callers." One night, Alex, Big E, myself, and Jack, the debate champ at UNM and also the debate coach at Academy high school, the most exclusive private school in the state, went out. We were a strange looking crew. Alex was a huge white boy with short hair. Big E was an even bigger black guy who weighed around three hundred pounds. Then there was Jack who had a neo-hippie look going, including a tie-dyed shirt and sandals. Then there was me. I had long hair braided into a ponytail and a long goatee. I wore baggy pants and a Pendleton shirt. I had been up on cocaine and alcohol for several days.

We walked into the bathroom and I pulled a sock with about forty papers and a quarter ounce in a plastic bag out of my pants. My procedure was to stuff the dope into the sock and then stick the sock down my pants and tie it to my belt. This prevented it from falling out and made it difficult to locate if I was patted down.

We got high in the bathroom and then walked out with white powder all over our hands and faces. As we walked across the dance floor like we owned the place, some girl came up and said "hi" to me. That is the last thing I remember. I went into a drug induced seizure and did *the fish* right there on the dance floor. When I regained consciousness, I was surrounded by a crowd of people. Alex was in the crowd and got my attention. He signaled to remind me that I had the drugs in my pants. Shortly after, the paramedics arrived and talked with me for a bit. I told them I suffered from seizures, but that was a lie. This was my first one but not the last. Later I found out that the girl who had come up to talk to me had wanted to party that night, but since she saw me flopping like a fish on the dance floor she stopped doing drugs. Sometimes, unexpectedly, something good comes out of something bad.

As mentioned earlier, the rap music we listened to glorified the life we lived. The music influenced me in a stronger way than I realized. I am not saying that the music made me what I had become, but it did play a part. Listening to those lyrics over and over had an effect. There is power in the tongue to bring life or death. That music was all about pride, violence, drugs, disrespecting women, and street respect. I began to believe what the music was saying. I had become a pawn on Satan's chess board. I believe Satan anoints musicians to promote wickedness in the same way the Holy Spirit anoints musicians to promote holiness.

Life had brought me to a destination of success and respect on the streets, or so I thought at the time. I was popular. Girls liked me and guys feared me, but I was still incredibly lonely and cocaine had made me anti-social. I could not even be around people I did not know unless I was completely drunk or stoned. Many times I wished it would all end, but it just wouldn't go away.

Big-E ended up getting pulled over with thirty thousand dollars in cash and some rock. The police took his pager, the money, and his phones. The narcotics officers began trying to bust others by answering the phones and pager. Big-E got out of jail on bail and warned us to turn off our pagers and stop dealing drugs because the cops were onto us.

Alex ended up moving into my house because his apartment was hot (the cops were watching it). Rather than stop, Alex started to get cocaine from me and we served Big-E's clients. We would drive by the crack houses and drop off product. With Big-E out of the picture we were the suppliers for several other neighborhoods. We were always "strapped" (carrying a gun) for protection. When Alex moved in things got even crazier. There were more clients and more drugs. That's when I started leaving my own house to stay in hotels. I had no peace. I was continually nervous and high. I could not even enjoy my "success." It was like I was in a bad movie that would not end. I didn't know it, but my little kingdom was about to be really shaken.

Chapter 3

BUSTED

My life spiraled out of control. Paranoia devastated me, stole any peace and joy I might have had, and left me a wreck. I did not want this life anymore, but I felt trapped. Walls of pain surrounded me that became so strong I felt as though I was in a literal prison. I was a shell of a man.

We now had twice the traffic, and I saw that Alex had become a jerk. I watched how he treated people, and then I realized I did the exact same thing. I did not comprehend the horror of my actions until I saw them through another person. Alex had played for the UNM football Lobos until the coach kicked him off the team for using steroids and selling drugs to the other players. One day, as we left to handle "business," Jack, who watched the house while I was gone said, "I called Alex by his last name and Alex whirled around and said, 'Don't ever call me that! Only friends call me that." Jack had a scared look on his face.

Alex could be very intimidating. He treated everyone like they were the valet parking attendants looking for a tip, and I acted the same. When everyone is continually groveling it just becomes natural. It's a role to play, but there was some tension developing in this drama.

There was an older guy who was introduced to me by one of Tristan's friends. My connection had not come in from Mexico, and I needed a couple of pounds of marijuana immediately, so I met this guy's father. I picked up the weed, and I used to carry a bullet filled with cocaine. A bullet is a vial with a cap that looks like a real bullet, and you can turn it over, load up a hit in the reservoir, and then put it to your nose and snort. I always had a full vial and I had it when the deal went down. I asked the father if he wanted a rail, but he said no, he had a problem with the stuff. Once he started doing it he would not stop. I told him, "My weed connect will be back soon, so I won't need to see you for this again (he charged too much anyway), but if you ever need anything, you can just page me." He soon called every weekend and then every few days. This went on for a while and is an example of how things can get out of hand.

One afternoon I picked up a book of acid (ten sheets, or one thousand hits). I decided to take a few hits and go to the Sandia Mountains and relax for a while. I had even given Alex my pager, cell phone, and drugs so he could handle business for me. Things got busy and I ended up not leaving right away. I had several deliveries to make. Then a friend paged me with a code that said he needed an ounce. When I called him back he actually said over the phone, "I need eight 8-balls." (An ounce has eight eighths which weigh 3.5 grams each.) This violated my rules against talking business on the phone; however, at this point the acid was totally kicking in. I was tripping so hard that I did not catch on to what he had done until later. I did notice it, and it seemed weird, but I thought maybe I was just paranoid and tripping because I actually was tripping on acid.

That night as I, under the influence of psychedelics, saw all the madness, it really did seem like a bad drug movie. Piles of cocaine and marijuana sat on my coffee table with a triple beam and a HK 9mm pistol next to the scale. What was going on with my life? I decided to meet my friend at the 66 Diner, right down the street from my house, to give him the ounce and get the money he owed me.

I told Alex to drive me to do this deal. I grabbed the gun and a briefcase with about a quarter kilo of cocaine. Alex said, "Leave the *gat* and product here." He was right, so I left it and he drove me to the diner because I was tripping too hard to drive. We circled it once to check it out, then he dropped me off. I went over to the Camaro that my friend drove and got in the passenger seat. He had a nervous look on his face and acted weird. Again, I thought it was just the acid affecting me. I handed him the cocaine, and he handed me the money. He said, "That extra five hundred I owe you is there, too." I said, "Okay good," acting like I remembered what he owed me. I had a debt book in my briefcase with over a hundred names of people who owed me money, but could not remember who owed what without checking it.

After handing me the money, he pumped his brakes several times, and then six cars came from all over and surrounded his vehicle. It was the undercover narcotics division. I was busted. They pulled me out of the car and began to quiz me. They even tried the good cop, bad cop routine. It was almost funny because I was tripping out on how each man played his role. At this point, I was peaking on acid and did not know if this was really happening. The cops told me that if I hooked up a deal for a quarter kilo right then, I would not go to jail. I responded with an attitude. I said, "I'm no snitch. Take me to jail. The sooner I get there, the sooner I get out." They confiscated my brand new red Mitsubishi Eclipse, and they kept it by saying it had been purchased with drug money.

They let Alex go since he did not have any dope on him, and they had no information about him. He played "the dumb jock" and it worked. Everyone, including the cops, loved the UNM football players. A black-and-white cop car was called and they took me downtown, and all the while I was tripping hard on the acid. I was booked for trafficking cocaine and possession of LSD. To add insult to injury, I was taken into a small room and strip-searched. They checked every crevice of my body and even had me bend over and cough. This would have been horrible for anyone, but it was accentuated by the fact that I was on LSD. They had taken all my money, so I could not bail out. I would have to stay in jail until Monday morning to see a judge. I was taken to my cell at Bernalillo County Detention Center (BCDC).

The jail was overcrowded and the cells were small. I curled up on the floor next to the toilet to sleep because I was tripping so bad. I barely slept, if I slept at all. I was with two older guys, a black guy who got busted with a couple of rocks in the war zone, and a Hispanic guy who got busted carrying a stolen television down the street. He was on his way to get some heroin. He was what we called a *tecato* (male heroin junkie).

We talked for a while in Spanish. They asked me what my charges were and I said cocaine trafficking. When I mentioned it was for an ounce of cocaine, they were both in shock. "That's a lot of dope, man!" the black guy said. To me that was not a lot of product because I was moving so much weight. These guys were street junkies who lived from fix to fix. I remember thinking "these guys are losers. Walking down the street with a stolen television: how stupid could you be!" What I did not know was that one day I would be in the same condition. I did not eat all weekend and actually got some sleep on Sunday. I called my father and he said he would come to court on Monday.

Afterwards, I called my house to tell them to clean it up. A guy named Chris answered my phone and I told him to get Jason, my next door neighbor. He left and came right back to the phone saying undercover cops were at Jason's house, but they had not come to my house. I told him to get the drugs and guns out of my house. He was very scared and said he was taking off. I called back about an hour later and Tristan answered. He said Jason's house got raided and they took his marijuana plants. They had come to Jason's door asking for me. For some reason they had been told that Jason's was my house. Later, I found out that Alex had told them that so they wouldn't go to my house and find the kilo and firearms. Jason later told me he thought I had "snitched him out" at first, but then realized that they thought it was my house. After that, he just kept his mouth shut, which is what the "code" says one is supposed to do. Jason obeyed the rules.

Tristan told me that Alex came back and had cleaned out the house and had my drugs and guns and was going to raise my thirty-thousand-dollar bond and get me out. He did not come up with all the money, and I stayed in jail. Tristan said he had paged me with his code and a 911 to tell me that my friend who had set me up to be busted had his house raided. The "friend" had also snitched on two other people. He set us all up. Everyone has an aversion to people who sell others out to save their own hides. Getting his house raided was his own fault. He would let his son, who was a senior in high school, have parties with underage kids drinking, using, and buying drugs. Eventually someone's parents called the cops, and for good reason. I smugly patted myself on the back. I did not sell drugs to kids, and I didn't rat on people. I figured I was a saint compared to that "lowlife."

But, the Bible warns us not to compare ourselves to other humans, only to God. When it comes to our relationships with Him "all [of us] have sinned and fallen short of the glory of God" (Romans 3:23). Realizing how we compare to a pure and holy God is our first step toward salvation. Of course, that is another huge biblical truth of which I was not aware.

Monday morning I went into the courtroom and my dad was brought in when it was my turn to stand before the judge. This was my first adult charge. When the judge saw my father she granted me a Third Party Release. The judge had known my father and our family for many years and trusted him to make sure I showed up in court. My father picked me up when I was released, and I asked to go to my house. He said he was responsible for me going to court. I said I would go to court, but I wanted to go home. He refused to go to my house, so I told him to let me out of the car. He stopped at a gas station and I thanked him. I got out and called Alex for a ride home.

The police had seized my Mitsubishi, but I still had a beat-up 1968 Volkswagen van. Fortunately, the narcs had gone to the wrong house or I would have been in much worse trouble. This was a crossroads in my life, but I didn't realize it. I could have sought treatment for my addiction and continued my college career; however, I did not. I withdrew from my third semester of UNM classes without contacting the professors, so I failed all of them. After the bust, my landowner kicked me out of the house. I went back to military school (NMMI) for one semester, and my father helped me to get one of the best attorneys in town.

I was so apathetic, jaded, and beaten down that the darkness around me grew deeper. I was so delusional from the cocaine, alcohol, and Valium that I could not even talk straight. I would mumble so badly that people could not understand me. It would have been funny if it were not so pathetic. A friend of mine, Mike, drove me around to deliver drugs. He was one of the few people who could understand my mumbling. It became a joke that he was my official translator.

I just wanted the madness to somehow end. Later, I had a deep understanding of what the Apostle Paul meant when he wrote, "I do not understand my own actions. For I do not do what I want, but I do the very thing I hate" (Romans 7:15). I wanted to stop, but there was some desire deep within me driving me to do drugs and live the street life. It was obvious that there was no future in it. I was facing prison time and still could not get out of the cycle. Complete insanity.

Back to New Mexico Military Institute

It was the early '90s, and I spent several years fighting the cocaine trafficking charges. My dad convinced me to go back to NMMI because it would look good to the judge. I can't imagine what my father must have gone through during those years. He thought if I went back to military school, I would get better. That was not the case. I went back for a semester, but continued in my addiction. I would drive to Albuquerque on weekends and supply the people who sold dope for me with enough drugs to last the week, then take a stash back to NMMI to party.

At school, I became friends with Al Demeo. We talked, and I told him that I was a dope dealer that had gotten busted and that I had come back to NMMI to make a good impression on the judge. Later, he moved to Albuquerque to be my right hand man. When he came to town and saw my operation he admitted that he had doubted my story was true. He said, "Caleb you're one of

the few people I've met that talks the talk and walks the walk."
At the time, I took that as a compliment. Today, I pray that I am
a Christ-follower who talks the talk *and* walks the walk. I failed
most of my classes that time around at NMMI. I would stay up
all night doing cocaine in the dark in my room. After classes,
Lee, a friend of mine, and I would go pick up beer and drive
around while we got drunk. I was so relieved when that semester
came to an end.

Campus Street House with Jason

I moved back to Albuquerque and got a house with Jason,
the guy who lived next door to me when I got busted. He was
the guy whose house had been raided by accident. I sold major
amounts of drugs again.

Pedro started coming around and gave me some big customers.
One guy he brought was Richard Besgrove. He wanted a quarter
kilo, but this was the first time I had met him. I asked him if he
had the money and he showed me five thousand dollars cash.
I did not deal with him that day, but eventually we did a lot
of business. Richard owned several houses and an apartment
complex, all left to him by his parents. He had a speed boat,
and his house was decked out. He was busted several times with
large amounts of cocaine, but always got off with high-powered
attorneys. He ended up being one of my financial backers in
the dope game for a season. Years later he lost everything and
went insane. He received government assistance and lived on
the streets as a methhead; a very sad illustration of what dope
can do.

Jason had some girls who would come and clean the house
for a little dope. One of these girls was Heather. Her father was
a local architect and her parents were strict Mormons. Heather
moved in with me and started doing lots of cocaine. She loved
to do cocaine and would not want to stop. I would get scared

because she did so much that she would shake uncontrollably. Still, she wanted to do more.

One night, after we had a seventy-two hour binge, I told her we needed to get some sleep because we were starting to hallucinate from sleep deprivation. I took my usual fifty milligrams of Valium ("five blues"), a swig of Jack Daniels and coke, and a fat doobie (marijuana cigarette). I talked her into taking a couple of blues and gave her some Jack and coke so she would stop *jonesing* (craving) and pass out. We both eventually fell asleep. I remember waking up in the middle of the night and seeing her asleep with a cigarette in the bed. I said, "Put that out, Heather," and went back to sleep.

Later, I got up and stumbled into the back yard and lay down on one of the couches around a little fire pit we dug out of the desert. When I woke up again I saw flames coming out of my windows. I ran inside but could not get to my room because of the intense heat in the hallway. My friend Al was asleep on the couch in the living room. I told him to get up because the house was on fire. He opened his eyes and looked at me. Then he turned over to go back to sleep. I went and slapped him and yelled, "Fire!"

Again, fearing that Heather was still there, I tried to get to my room. I needed to save her! I was unable to get to the room, so I went around to the front of the house to get up to my second bedroom window. There was Heather with the garden hose trying to spray the flames. It was almost comical because there was no pressure. She had put her thumb over the head to increase the pressure, to no avail. Barely a dribble was coming out. I grabbed her and took her to the front of the house where a passerby stopped and said he had called the fire department.

The fire department showed up and put out the fire. While the local news cameras were shooting footage gunshots could be clearly heard from the handgun ammunition inside the house.

After the fire was put out, I asked to go in to get cash that was in my room. I went to the foot of my bed where I kept my money and all that was left of the nearly twenty thousand dollars in cash were some partially burned one hundred dollar bills. I owed most of the money because I had gotten a front on some cocaine. I went to the guy who loaned me the money and told him the money had burned. He looked at me disdainfully and said, "Really?" I showed him a plastic bag filled with partly burned bills. Next I went to the bank where I was able to turn in burned bills with partial serial numbers remaining. I salvaged about two thousand dollars. This was devastating; I had lost almost everything I owned in the world. The last letter my grandma wrote me before passing away was gone. Everything was gone.

Later, Heather and I would have a daughter, Ashli, together. Heather moved to Utah with Ashli and got married. Her husband adopted Ashli and allowed me no contact until she was eighteen. Ashli is in college now and is a great girl, but we only have a cordial relationship. One of my biggest regrets is not being in her life. There are consequences to our actions. I spread a wake of devastation for everyone I knew, especially those who dared to love me.

The only time I would see any college friends was when they came to buy drugs. Everything was now out in the open and my family knew for certain about my secret life. Instead of getting better, I got worse. The cocaine was driving me mad. I did cocaine nonstop and was drinking heavily to balance out the paranoia from the coke. The paranoia was now accentuated by the recent bust. I thought there were police behind every bush. I had people drive me around to drop off drugs, and we would do more dope at every stop. I carried a fifth of Jack Daniels with me everywhere.

I mixed Valium with the alcohol to try and level myself out, and I took the blues like they were candy: ten milligrams every few hours mixed with the alcohol. Often, I would overdo and wake up after being passed out at a customer's house or in my car.

My life was out of control. I had always stayed away from heroin because I had some family members that had struggled with that addiction. Again, I thought people who used needles were losers. A girl I sold dope to was a pharmacist at the local hospital. She was also a heroin addict. She would pick up cocaine from me and mix it with the heroin and shoot it. She gave me some and I tried to snort it but didn't really feel it.

Another friend of mine, Nathan, had been using heroin for some time. He was the son of a pastor in Albuquerque. One night I dropped off some cocaine to him and some of his friends. I asked him if he had any clean needles and some heroin. He said, "Of course, Caleb. Do you want some?"

I said, "Yeah, I think I want to try it so it will mellow out the coke, but I don't know how to shoot up. Can you hit me?"

"You got it bro!" he said.

Nathan went through the little ritual of cooking the dope and pulling it into the syringe. He then shot me up for the first time. I had him shoot me up for the next few days, but I quickly caught on and began shooting up myself. Speedballs (cocaine and heroin taken intravenously) became my new best friends and even my gods. Heroin interacted with the cocaine in such a way that I no longer became paranoid from the coke. It was a "miracle drug."

Nathan had been strung out on heroin for several years. One day he dropped by my house and asked if he could use my .45 caliber handgun.

"What do you want it for?" I asked.

"Just to use for a few hours"

"No!" I said. "You're just going to get yourself in trouble, and if you do something stupid you're going to get me in trouble."

It just did not feel right. Nathan was a great guy, but he was not hardcore. He was not the type to carry a gun or make enemies. He was a fun-loving guy. He went to every rave and loved to dance all night. He was the life of the party, but just not a thug. He left and later that week we saw on the news that Nathan had been shot in the back by the police while robbing the Subway restaurant across from UNM, a few blocks from my house. He had robbed it twice in the same week and went back a third time, but when he did the police were waiting. He had been using a plastic gun.

Nathan was paralyzed from the waist down. When he got out of the hospital he stayed at his parents' house, but was eventually kicked out for throwing wild parties. He got money and all kinds of pills from the government for being paralyzed. He sold his pills to support his heroin addiction. After a while, I lost contact with him, but about a year later we saw in the news that Nathan had overdosed with a prostitute in his room at a cheap hotel on Central Street. He became just another victim of the streets.

I continued to do heroin and my habit worsened. I was eventually put on probation for cocaine trafficking. I was given a conditional discharge which meant that if I finished the three years of probation successfully, the felony charge would fall off my record. Still, I gave a dirty urine sample to the probation officer (PO) almost every time he gave me a urinalysis (UA). In the meantime, to satisfy my probation requirements I enrolled back at UNM.

The Meadows in Wickenburg, Arizona

I continued to drop dirty UAs to my probation officer. He mandated outpatient drug counseling to no avail. Then, he and my drug counselor had an intervention which required me to go through an inpatient drug rehab. My insurance through my father was with Blue Cross Blue Shield and they covered most of the thirty thousand dollars for the one-month stay at The Meadows, owned by Pia Mellody, a highly regarded expert in the fields of addiction and recovery. It is one of the best rehab facilities in the nation. I flew out there and had a few drinks at the airport and did the month-long program. When they dropped me back at the airport I started drinking before I even boarded the plane. When I got to Albuquerque my friends picked me up and we went to get high. I continued to be a hopeless junkie.

Teen Challenge Pig Farm in Spokane

One night I was driving back to my apartment from a downtown bar and I had a 8-ball of cocaine on me. I was driving drunk and in a hurry to get back to my pad to get high. I did not notice that I was speeding. I got pulled over and arrested after failing the drunk driving road test. The officer searched my car and found the bag of coke in my jacket, but threw it back into the car. I guess she felt like a DWI was enough for that night. I went to jail and they impounded my car. Upon my release, the coke was still there in my back seat. When my PO found out he was not happy to say the least.

I was required to enter a long term rehab and ended up going to a Teen Challenge rehab in Spokane, Washington. My dad called them and set it up. I think he thought the only way I could make it was to get me as far away from Albuquerque as possible. I was sent to jail for a few days for violating probation with the DWI and agreed to go to the inpatient rehab at Teen Challenge to get out of jail. My dad drove me up there. I smoked cigarettes at every stop because I knew I would have to quit once I arrived.

After a couple of days of driving, we pulled into the rehab. It was literally a rural pig farm. We worked all day long with pigs, just like the prodigal son in the Bible. We attended chapel daily and church on Sundays. I hated it. Of course, I was just there because I had to be. I thought about getting high every day. I did not have a "burning bush" experience at this time, but I did start to have moments of clarity. This was the Lord gradually drawing me back. I spent several months there before another guy and I got kicked out.

We were dropped off at the airport. I headed to Phoenix with the other guy. We had plans of getting wasted upon arrival and then making some money selling drugs. However, Teen Challenge had notified my probation officer that I was kicked out of the program and had been dropped off at the airport. I was arrested at the airport and spent the next few months in the Spokane County Jail.

Finally, my parole officer allowed me to get out because Teen Challenge agreed to take me back. When I arrived they informed me that I would be on a no-contact contract, which meant that I could not talk to anyone for thirty days. I agreed, but could not handle it. I finally went to the director and told him I wanted to leave. I called my PO and he said I could come back to New Mexico. When I got back I decided I would not do hard drugs, but would not give up drinking.

When I first got back I drove around town and everywhere I went that day I overheard people talking about Jesus, or God. I felt like God was after me. My heart was literally hurting because the conviction of the Holy Spirit was so strong upon me. It was like God was saying, "I am here and I want you to stay with me." But, my mind was made up. I still wanted to "party" and have "fun," but I would stay away from hard drugs. I drove east on a one way street from I-25 towards the student "ghetto" which was my old stomping grounds. I passed the community college (CMN) on my right heading toward Yale Street. I felt as though God was literally in the car asking me to not leave Him. I tried to ignore Him, but his presence was overwhelming. The cars in front of me and next to me all had Christian bumper stickers, and they stood out as if highlighted by the universe. There is no way this is a coincidence, I thought.

Then, I came to the light at Yale and Lead Streets. I looked up and there was a huge billboard right there on the corner, and it was a picture of Jesus with his arms open. It had been put there by the Catholic church and had been there for years, but that day it was if Jesus himself was standing before me with open arms saying, "Come to me, John Caleb, and I will give you rest for your soul."

That was too much! I felt like I was going to have a heart attack. I could barely drive. I pulled over at the next street and prayed, "God, if this is you please leave me alone. I don't want you right now."

I calmed down and then drove away. Eventually, the presence left and things were back to the way they had always been. However, in my heart I knew that God had tried to prevent me from going back to all the madness and sin. The Lord is gracious. He was revealing himself to me like I had prayed for him to do many years before. Lamentably, despite the conviction of the Holy Spirit, I continued down the path of my choosing.

My life could have been changed forever at that time if I would have surrendered. But, I was in my early twenties and still loved the world, and my hedonistic lifestyle. I had only about a year left on probation. To satisfy my probation officer, I got a job at MCI as a Spanish-speaking representative. About six months later, my probation officer released me from probation, but I had lost my conditional discharge because of the DWI. The felony trafficking charges would remain on my permanent record. As soon as I found I did not have to report to my parole officer anymore, I started doing cocaine, heroin, and weed again. I ended up getting fired from work for missing too many days and started back with my full-time criminal lifestyle.

Chapter 4

STUPIDER, LAS VEGAS AND BEYOND

I started drinking heavily and doing heroin and cocaine again. My life quickly got out of control. I started selling drugs and was involved with people who were doing identity theft. My friend Mike A. was the identity theft king in New Mexico. We spent a lot of time together because we were both heroin addicts and we quickly developed a close relationship. I moved in with a girl, Tara, from Kentucky. She wanted to shoot drugs with me. I told her it would destroy her life and would not let her. I finally gave in, and she started doing heroin and cocaine intravenously from day one.

One weekend we were planning on going to Las Vegas. Las Vegas is an eight-hour drive, or a forty-five-minute flight from Albuquerque. Throughout the years, I would go to "Sin City" often. I loved to gamble and live it up in Las Vegas. I was never very good at gambling, but kept trying. Pedro and I were actually in Las Vegas at Bally's when the Dunes hotel was imploded. Bally's is across the street from the Dunes. We watched it fall from our window at Bally's on October 27, 1993. My life was imploding just like the Dunes as I continued my destructive lifestyle.

At any rate, Tara and I made plane and hotel reservations. We then went on a binge for the last twelve hours before our flight left. I ended up overdosing on heroin in our apartment. Tara called the paramedics, and I awoke in the hospital. I remember being angry with Tara for calling the paramedics because I did not want them to bust me. When I awoke though she was there with me at the hospital.

She said, "I am going to cancel our trip because our plane leaves in one hour."

I said, "What are you talking about?"

It took some convincing, but they let me leave the hospital. We made it to the airport just in time. We flew first class so we took advantage of the free drinks. I decided it would be a Bloody Mary kind of weekend and I drank non-stop on the flight.

We arrived at our hotel in Las Vegas and called for a limo. We went out to an expensive restaurant where the bill, including alcohol, was more than five hundred dollars. We then went to the casino and got tickets to watch *An Evening at the Improv.* I was drunk. Tara and I got into an argument and she took off with my wallet and room key in her purse. I walked down the strip to our hotel and got into our room and passed out. When she got back to the room she asked why I had left. She said, "I told you I was going to the bathroom." We ended up arguing again, and I threw the television, smashing the window. Security came and arrested me. I told her to take off and that I did not ever want to see her again. I was put in jail and still didn't have my wallet. She went back to Albuquerque, and, now sober, I called her the following day.

I said, "What are you doing?"

She replied. "You told me to leave."

I then said, "Well, I'm in jail, and you have my wallet, money, and credit cards. Come back and get me out of jail."

She got on the next flight and came and bailed me out. We paid the hotel for the damages and they dropped the charges.

We went to a different hotel because the first one had banned us. The next day we got married at the infamous Little White Chapel. When we got back to New Mexico she said she did not want me hanging out with my friends anymore. We broke up in a few weeks and she went back to Kentucky and filed for divorce.

I spent a lot of time with Mike A. We sold drugs and did identity theft to support our thousands of dollars per week habits of heroin and cocaine (speedballs). We got pounds of meth from my Mexican connections. The meth was called *shards*, *ice*, or *glass*. This was the mid-'90s. The feds started putting limitations on the materials to cook meth; however, this did not limit the amount of meth on the streets. At this time, the Mexican super labs started producing an enormous amount of the product. Meth became more popular than cocaine and heroin. My life was out of control as usual. Also as usual, I wanted the madness to end, but did not know how to stop it. The pain from withdrawal from heroin was horrendous. I would rather be dead than experience that. I was dead though in a living, walking dead kind of way.

Mike A. died in 2007. He shot up heroin in a hot bath. Junkies use hot baths to get their veins up. After shooting up, he "nodded out" and sank under the water and drowned.

Angel in the Back Seat

At one point, a girl I was dating went back to the Twin Cities to visit her parents for a few weeks. While she was gone I drove around making deliveries by myself and one day pulled over at a gas station on the corner of Coal Street and I-25. I got out the bottom of a coke can and cooked up a chunk of black tar heroin. I filled up a one cc syringe to the top. It took me a while to find a vein, but I finally did and then after shooting up I got on the freeway headed north.

Shortly after, I realized I had done too much. I began to "nod out" (pass out from heroin) on the freeway. I almost went off the road before I woke up and pulled back onto the highway. Since there was a lot of traffic I quickly snapped out of it because I feared I would die if I did not stay awake. I thought surely I would not pass out now because the adrenaline was pumping, but a few minutes later I nodded out again. I began to pull off the freeway and plunge off an overpass when a voice from the back seat called my name.

"John!"

I woke up and thought it was my girlfriend, but she was in Minneapolis and I was alone in the car. In my mind's eye, I thought I saw an angel in the back seat. I became very scared and pulled off the freeway at Lomas Street, the next exit. Once I got on Lomas Street I again nodded out and ran into the back of a truck while only going forty miles per hour, not the freeway speed of seventy.

No one got injured, but my hood was smashed almost to the windshield. Fortunately the car I drove had an automatic seat belt that pulled over the driver when the door shut. I got out of the car and fell to the ground. The belt left a bruise across my chest for a month, but I lived. I could have killed myself or, even worse, someone else, even an innocent child. During this period of my life, high on dope, I totaled four cars. To this day, I can still hear that angelic voice that saved my life on the freeway.

Years later, while in prison at the facility in Los Lunas, I was watching "GOD TV." There was a show hosted by Cindy Jacobs called, "God Knows." It was a program about angels. Before the show started that day, I was thinking, "I wonder if that really was an angel that called my name on the freeway, saving my life?" As soon as the show began, Cindy turned to the camera and said, "Just now someone is wondering if that was an angel that saved his life from an accident on the freeway many years ago, and God says, "Yes, yes it was." Wow! I felt goose bumps over my entire body and thanked God for his grace and mercy upon my life.

Throughout the years, I had a great friend named Joe. He sold high grade marijuana that he grew down in the South Valley. He drank a lot and smoked weed, but didn't do hard drugs. A few times he would call me up for a few grams of coke to "party" with a girl, but not often. One evening we were partying and he had some cocaine with him. He asked if I would do some with him. I said, "I only shoot it, I don't snort it." He said, "Come on just snort some with an old friend." So I did. We did a lot of coke that night.

Toward the morning we wanted to come down and head home. I had some bars of Xanax and some Valium. I gave him several bars and some Valium but instructed him to take only one pill. At about 7:00 a.m. we left the North Valley where we were partying. I went home to go to sleep. He had invited me to come to his parents' house in the South Valley, but I was too out of it to go. He went to his parents' house for breakfast that morning. I had taken several pills and slept all day Sunday until around 3:00 a.m. on Monday.

On Monday at 8:00 a.m., I went back to my job at MCI. Someone called my job to tell me that Joe had flipped his car coming back from his parents' house and had died. I was heartbroken. I just knew he had taken more pills than he should have and had passed out. Throughout the years, I lost sixteen friends to the streets. Most were overdoses to heroin, three were shootings, and one was from a car accident.

I left work and picked up a bottle of Jack Daniels. I was on my way to the west side to see my friend Jeff. On I-40 some little punks in a car were throwing up signs. I threw up a sign back at them and kept going. They kept on so I followed them to a Walgreens where they parked. I took a bottle out of the back seat and broke it to use as a weapon and went after the carload of guys. They hunkered down in the car and called the police. The police showed up quickly, and I was arrested for a DWI.

Victory Outreach in Denver

In the early part of 1998, I was convicted of commercial burglary. I was given a deal by the judge if I would enter a program for at least one year. I did not report because I was strung out on heroin and didn't want to go through the withdrawals. I finally consented to let my dad drive me to a rehab called Cynicore in Denver, Colorado. On the drive, I began to go through horrible withdrawals including cold sweats, shakes, and body pains so excruciating that death would be a relief. When we arrived in Denver I was taken to the emergency room where they said I was dehydrated. They hooked me up to an IV and I was then taken to Denver CARES Detox to kick heroin. I spent another week there in pain and with sleepless nights. When I was finally feeling better I called my girlfriend back in Albuquerque and had her bring a quarter ounce of heroin and a half ounce of cocaine. She picked me up at the rehab and we went to a hotel and did drugs for a week. I overdosed several times.

When the dope was gone she went back to Albuquerque quickly because within hours she would be kicking heroin and we didn't have a connection in Denver. I remember when she left she did not even look back. I believe she cared about me, but cared about heroin much, much more. In fact, I was even more worried about kicking the heroin myself than I was about her. I sat there in that lonely hotel room knowing I had to be out by noon that day.

What had become of my life? I was so lonely and scared I felt like my life was over. Remembering an earlier suggestion of my dad's, I impulsively decided to go to a Christian rehab by the name of Victory Outreach in Denver. They came and picked me up from the hotel, and I went to the rehab. I spent several months there.

A bunch of guys lived there and ate together in the huge house. At that rehab home, I met guys who had lived a life of crime and drugs but had found freedom in Jesus Christ. Of course, I had known about Jesus, having been born into my Christian family. I knew a lot about Jesus and religion, but did not know Jesus. Each morning we would wake up at 5:00 a.m. and go to an outside room where we stayed for an hour to pray. I remember thinking I would give it a try since I had to be in the room for an hour anyhow. I prayed for everything I could think of including family, friends, world peace, and even starving children in third-world countries. At the end of all my praying, I looked at my watch and only five minutes had passed.

"How do these guys do this?" I thought. Prayer was a real struggle.

We went three times a week to a church that was across the street. During the days, we did chores around the church and house. It was an interesting environment, but I still was holding back because I wanted to be on the streets doing drugs with my girlfriend. One day I got into an argument with one of the staff and packed my bags and took a bus back to Albuquerque. My girlfriend picked me up, and we went back to her apartment and got high. She was staying at the apartment of a couple that owed me a lot of money. They refused to pay, so I told my girlfriend to take some of their things to a pawn shop to cover their debt.

Later that night, Joe, the guy from the couple that owed me the money, drove by my girlfriend and me as we were waiting for a connection outside a 7-Eleven convenience store on the corner of Montgomery and Carlisle Streets. Joe drove slowly and looked over at us. He then turned around and drove into the 7-Eleven parking lot. He was with the girl, a stripper, who was living with him. She and my girlfriend did not get along.

They pulled up and Connie, the stripper, said, "Joe is going to kill you, Caleb."

He got out of the car, and I told him to get back in and drive away, but Connie kept instigating so he rushed at me. Twice I told him to step back. When he continued to rush me, I stabbed him in the chest with a knife, and he fell to the ground. My girlfriend and I ran out into an alley, threw the knife away, and went to another gas station to meet the connection. By the grace of God, Joe did not die. He was released later that night from the hospital.

Phoenix Victory Outreach

Now, not only had I left a court appointed rehab and violated probation, but also had been involved in a stabbing. Albuquerque was not a good place for me to stay. Drug trafficking was a tough business, and I had made some enemies that would just as soon shoot me as look at me.

I had planned on going to Mexico to beat the charges. We drove to Phoenix intending to go south from there. However, I knew we would not stay on the run very long if we were still getting high (riding dirty). I needed to get off the *chiva* (black tar heroin). Victory Outreach had a facility in Phoenix so my girlfriend and I entered the Phoenix Victory Outreach.

I knew the madness had to end. I could not continue the same lifestyle. My girlfriend went into the women's home, and I went into the men's home under an alias. This was on a Monday. I spent a week in bed once again kicking heroin. It was not as bad because I had only been back on the street for few months or so.

That Thursday was Thanksgiving day, 1998, and there was a church service and dinner for the men's and women's homes. At church, I did not see my girlfriend and found out she had left that same night we checked in. She could not handle the withdrawals from the heroin. She went back home and ended up being with my best friend, Mike A. He was a meth dealer and thief and always had a lot of money. I felt betrayed, but I had left because of my own problems and had to deal with my issues. They tried to hide it from me, but I just knew and some friends also told me. Even though I was on blackout and unable to have outside contact, I would occasionally make unapproved phone calls from a nearby pay phone.

During my first few months in Phoenix, I surrendered my life to Jesus Christ and began to trust in Him. God also began to reveal Himself to me. His presence was so tangible that even though I couldn't see Him with my natural eyes, I could see, and sense, Him with the eyes of my spirit. I was born again and my spiritual eyes were opened! I was aware of a whole other world that had always been there, but I was blind to it. I could not believe that it took me this long to find out that God was real. God had always been there knocking at the door of my heart, but I had closed Him out. My life of sin had separated me from Him. But, that had dramatically changed. I felt like I was actually inhabited by another being, and I was! God's Holy Spirit now lived within me (Ephesians 1:13-14).

I could hear a voice behind my voice and felt and knew that the Spirit of the Living God was in me. It is hard to speak of spiritual things in natural words, but I knew that God was real and He not only loved me, but He *liked* me. The God of the universe stooped down very low to meet a heroin junkie that the whole world had counted out. The Lord is gracious!

At Phoenix, we got up early and prayed for an hour then had a chapel service. After that, we would eat breakfast. Some of us would then stay and do chores around the house, while others went out to work for the day. We were busy all day and at the end of the day we were tired. This was ideal for me. I did not have time to think about getting high. Boredom was a "trigger" for me. I had to be active. Another thing I now had was purpose and a higher law. I was never afraid of the police again because I never had any reason to be.

When Christ came in and became Lord of my life I followed Him. My worldview changed overnight. A divine nature was replacing my sinful nature. I now would not steal or use drugs because I knew that displeased my Creator. My "factory settings" had been reset and I was a new creation. I was becoming the person God created me to be. I spent all my free time reading my Bible. I was hooked on the Bible and could read it for hours on end. It was "food" to my spirit. Jesus said, "I am the living bread that came down from heaven. If anyone eats of this bread he will live forever" (John 6:51). I felt my spirit getting stronger each day.

Not only would I not commit crime or do drugs because it would offend my God, but I did not even want that lifestyle anymore. My addictions were gone. I was a new creation. The old had gone and something brand new had come.

The Apostle Paul wrote in his letter to the church in Philippi, "For it is God who works in you, both to will and to work for his good pleasure" (Philippians 2:13). God wants to give us a new heart. He not only gives us the strength to do what pleases Him, but gives us the desire to do what pleases Him. In Psalms, it says, "Delight yourself in the LORD, and he will give you the desires of your heart" (Psalm 37:4). The Hebrew word, *delight*, means to "take great joy in the presence of." As we spend time in the Lord's presence, our hearts are changed. We begin to desire the things that He desires, and then He gives them to us. We get the desires of our heart when they line up with the heart of God. This was the promise of God through the Prophet Ezekiel: "I will give you a new heart, and a new spirit I will put within you. And I will remove the heart of stone from your flesh and give you a heart of flesh. And I will put my Spirit within you, and cause you to walk in my statutes and be careful to obey my rules" (Ezekiel 36:26-27). What Ezekiel wrote more than twenty-six centuries ago remains true for us today because God never changes. The Holy Spirit empowers us to gladly follow the Lord!

Chapter 5

THE CALL OF GOD; FINALLY I "GET IT"

At the beginning of 1999, all the men in the home went to a Southwest Regional Victory Outreach rehab conference in Glorieta, New Mexico, for the weekend. It was called the "Men of Conviction" conference. About five hundred men representing recovery homes from all over the southwest were there.

On the first night of the conference an evangelist named Phillip LaCrue spoke. The title of his message was, "The God of Second Chances." I don't remember the details of the message, but I do remember that at the end he made an altar call. He said that all those who felt that God had called them to full time ministry should answer that call by coming forward. This was a rehab conference and each man thought he was the next Billy Graham because he had been clean for a few months and prayed every morning. Almost everyone from the Phoenix men's home went forward. I stayed in my seat and told God, "I am not going forward unless you speak to me."

I will never forget what happened next. I felt the presence of God come over me from my head to my feet. I then began to weep like a little baby. I had not cried for as long as I could remember. Even as a child when my parents divorced, I did not cry. My little brother cried often, but I pushed everything inside. This was an uncontrollable weeping from deep within. I said,

"Okay, Lord," got out of my seat, and quickly walked to the front. As I looked at the altar, I saw what appeared to be a cloud, or mist, enveloping it. When I arrived at the altar, between sobs I began to speak in a language I had never learned before.

I was consumed with love for everyone around me. There were some knuckleheads at that conference (this author included), but I felt the love of God flowing in and out of me. I kept saying, "I love you guys," and meant it. This was not the same John I had always been. I was naturally critical and easily annoyed by those around me. Now the reality of the Kingdom of God and the glory of God's love was so tangible to me I had no doubt that God was with me and that He had called me into ministry.

That same weekend my dad drove up from Albuquerque to visit. He was so happy to see that this son of his who had been so lost was now found. I asked his forgiveness for the years of pain I had caused him, and he tearfully accepted my apology and said, "It was all worth it to see you now."

I went back to Phoenix Sunday afternoon with the ragtag crew of the men's home in our well-worn old van, and I felt like I was the happiest person on the face of the earth. God was not only real, but he stooped down so low as to meet me and call me into his service. I once heard a preacher say, "I was born again when I believed in God, but I was transformed when I found that He believes in me." I had been transformed that weekend at Glorieta!

I traveled back to Phoenix a totally different man. One of my jobs was to clean the bathrooms at the church. I scrubbed those toilets and left them sparkling. The guy on staff even told me, "They don't have to be perfect." But, yes they did! This was God's house and his toilets would shine if I had anything to do with it. No job was too low for me to do, and I did them all with such great joy! God was alive and living in me. I had purpose now. God not only loved me, but He actually liked me! I could feel his favor all day long. My thoughts would continually go up to God and we communed constantly.

After I completed the year-long Victory Outreach program, I served as staff at the youth home and men's home.

Do You Remember When We First Met?

Later, I went to the Victory Outreach School of Ministry (Urban Training Center) in Los Angeles. While at the School of Ministry we would often go street witnessing on Skid Row and Santa Monica Pier. One night when we were out after midnight we went to the Santa Monica Pier. I got separated from the group and looked over and saw a little shooting gallery like the one at Disneyland when I was four years old. As I stared at the gallery, the Lord spoke clearly to me, "Do you remember when we first met?" I broke down and began weeping. I said, "Yes, Lord, I remember." Although I left the Lord and forgot about Him, He never forgot about me. His mercy endures forever.

In your journey through life with all its struggles and problems, have you forgotten God? He has never forgotten you.

Missionary to the Philippines

After I completed the School of Ministry, I was asked to join a missionary team to Manila, the capital city of the Philippines. When I was asked to go, I let leadership know that I would need to pray about this because there was a possibility that I had charges pending for the stabbing in 1998. At that time, my father asked if I wanted to go with him to revival services at Brownsville Assembly of God in Pensacola, Florida. I decided to take a week and head over with my father to check it out. I had not heard anything about it and he only had some limited hearsay information. I kept an open mind to a word from God and prayed that He would give me guidance.

When we arrived there, the church parking lot was packed. I walked into the sanctuary and felt an awesome presence of God. I had not felt anything like that before. I did not know that this kind of power was available in God. The first night there some of the School of Ministry students (who had come in the van) asked me to go forward for prayer after the message. I declined, but they eventually convinced me. I walked down to the altar and Pastor Michael Brown laid one hand on my head and one on someone else's. I felt something incredible. An euphoric feeling more intense than anything I ever felt before came over me. The Spirit within me caught on fire and it felt great! Speedballs had been my drug of choice and I thought there was no greater high, until that evening. It was as if God was saying to me, "See, I've got the best of everything!"

In the Psalms, the author writes about God's presence: "You make known to me the path of life; *in your presence there is fullness of joy*; at your right hand are *pleasures forevermore*" (Psalm 16:11, italics mine).

The next night no one had to ask me to go forward. I was the first one up there, hands raised and eyes closed. The evening's experience was marvelous, but different in tone. The presence of God was so strong it was almost heavy. I love basking in the presence of God. The presence of God often comes at random times to me, perhaps while sitting in an airport, driving in my car, or just standing on a corner. Often his presence consumes and almost overwhelms me. His is a tangible presence that I feel deep within my being. It's like the Lord is lavishing his full love on me through the Holy Spirit. Sometimes, He comes to comfort me when I feel like I have failed. The Lord is always gracious. He knows none of us would make it without his holy, reassuring, and encouraging presence in our lives.

The revival evangelist, Steve Hill, was a former addict who had gone through the Teen Challenge program. I had heard of this program because that is where Sonny Arguinzoni, the founder of Victory Outreach, was saved in 1962. Sonny was reached by Pastor David Wilkerson and former gang member Nicky Cruz during the early days of Teen Challenge. He was set free from a heroin addiction and later came to Los Angeles and started the ministry of Victory Outreach, which plants churches through men's and women's recovery homes. I witnessed God using Steve in this mighty revival and I thought, "If God can use once hopeless drug addicts like Steve and Sonny, maybe He can use me, too."

There was a powerful spirit of repentance at this revival. People would run down to the altar and fall on their faces in repentance. They would leave their drugs on the altar. It was the most beautiful thing I had ever seen. I prayed that God would do that in my ministry also.

I had gone there seeking a word from God. The third night we went to a service featuring Prophet Johnny Foote, founder of Flame of Fire International. I asked the Lord, "Should I stay or should I go to Manila?"

I wanted to go as a missionary, but felt like I should go turn myself in to see if I had any pending charges. Either way, nothing would change. If I went to the mission field, I would serve Jesus. If I went to prison, I would still serve Jesus. As I was turning this over in my mind, Pastor Johnny motioned me up to the platform. He said, "God says go. You are not out of place, but in place." He then went on to say things about my past that there was no way he could have known. He also mentioned specifics about the future that have since happened. I was in shock. God had given me a direct answer to my question even though the future was yet to unfold. I went back to Los Angeles and a few weeks later left with the team for Manila.

In Manila, I was the Assistant Director of the School of Ministry (UTC). I also preached at our local churches and, with a team of students from the UTC, helped plant a church in Tondo, the worst neighborhood of metro Manila. God moved, and within six months we had over one hundred people attending. We did street evangelism and outreaches to *barangays* (neighborhoods) throughout Manila. We worked among the very poor, and addicts. There was much spiritual opposition, but demonized people were set free by the power of God.

After two years, our team headed back to the United States. When we arrived at Los Angeles International Airport (LAX), there was a long customs line. However, at the front of the line, I saw several customs agents with a picture in hand looking at everyone entering the country. I knew it was me they were looking for. When they got to me I had turned the other way. They asked me to look at them and when I did I saw the look of shocked recognition in their eyes. One of them said, "Sir, could you come with us?"

I said, "What seems to be the problem, officers?" They replied, "There's no problem. We're just taking you to the short line."

I said, "The short line, eh?"

It was a short line indeed! Just me. They arrested me for a fugitive warrant out of Albuquerque, New Mexico. I was taken to the LA County Jail. After about five months, I was extradited to Albuquerque to face charges. After being in the Bernalillo County Detention Center for several months, I was released to fight the charges. During my jail time, I had become discouraged. I was facing the possibility of more than twenty years in prison for the stabbing, absconding, receiving stolen property, and identity theft.

I started working for an insurance company and attending UNM again. Steadily, my daily time with the Lord dwindled to nothing. I slipped back into hanging out with my cousins and old friends. Lamentably, I eventually started shooting heroin again. I then was convicted of identity theft and receiving stolen property. When it came time for sentencing I decided to go on the lam. For the next year and a half, I was on the run from the law. I sold rock cocaine, methamphetamines, and heroin to support my addiction. I lived in cheap hotels. Many times I put a pistol to my head and thought about ending my life. I had failed everyone: my family; my God; and myself.

During this time, I was tormented by spiritual forces of evil. I would see and hear demons. Whether this was drug-induced or reality, I am not sure. What is for sure is that the enemy of my soul was working overtime to destroy me. He was up to one of his oldest and most effective tricks by separating me from my Christian brothers. The beast knows it is easier to destroy a lamb if it is separated from the flock.

The enemy could be working overtime in your life as well, trying to throw more junk into your path. Jesus' Apostle, Peter, warned about the enemy when he wrote, "Be sober-minded; be watchful. Your adversary the devil prowls around like a roaring lion, seeking someone to devour" (1 Peter 5:8). Peter goes on to write that we should resist the devil and stay firm in our faith. I had not done that and was easy prey.

Prison

In 2007, I was arrested and my face was all over the evening news, I was sent to prison to serve eight years. Although I had been on fire for God with mission work, church planting, and street witnessing, I was now far from God. I had cut myself off from Him and felt I was without any hope.

At the first facility I was at in Hobbs, New Mexico, my homies (friends) had an ongoing beef with some other guys there. One day a guy walked into my cell, supposedly to talk to my cell mate. I turned around for a second and he hit me with a sock that had a combination lock in it (a common weapon in prison). After a few minutes, I woke up with my head in a pool of blood.

I stumbled out of my cell and my homies quickly called for the corrections officer who called medical. I was taken to the prison doctor and stitched up. My friends later retaliated against the people we suspected of being the culprits. After that, we were all separated and sent to different facilities. I went to the toughest, the New Mexico State Penitentiary at Santa Fe. This was the site of the worst prison riot in US history in the 1980s.

I began getting narcotics into my new prison. I sold drugs and used drugs. I had my people out on the streets give drugs to girlfriends or wives of convicts and then they would bring the stuff to their boyfriends or husbands during visitation. They put the drugs in balloons so they could be swallowed. This worked for some time, until I was busted for dirty urine and a fresh tattoo. The officers suspected me of bringing narcotics into the facility, but they never caught me with any evidence. If I had been caught, I would have been facing possibly twenty extra years (eight years for habitual/twelve years for bringing narcotics into a state facility).

My Prison Became a Palace

In Santa Fe, I was sent to solitary confinement for five months. I walked into solitary in March, 2008. In this "hole" we were allowed no contact with others. We were allowed out only to shower for ten minutes on weekdays. In solitary confinement you can't receive books, but you can receive letters. Among other things, my dad sent me inspirational "letters" about the testimony of a young man who was a former addict that God used mightily. My dad would copy and send in ten pages at a time. When the guards pushed his envelopes under the door I would feel the presence of God in an incredible way. I would quake on my bed for hours, much like what I read about the early Quakers. If someone saw me, they might have thought I was in great pain. Not so! It may have looked painful, but on the contrary, it felt awesome. At times I would breathe out uncontrollably and I knew that God was setting me free from demons. In Manila, I saw people do the same thing when demons were cast out. They would arch their backs and exhale. You could almost see the demons leave.

I spent five months in that cell; just my Bible and me. I got down on my knees and cried out to God, "Lord Jesus, if you are still there, I need you! Would you please come back into my life and forgive me? I don't want to do anything great, I just want You back with the peace and joy that is found only in your presence."

God showed up. I felt his presence and knew He was with me. I repented and turned to Him again, this time with all my heart, mind, soul, and strength. All of me! I read my Bible eight to ten hours a day and prayed the rest of the day. I read the entire Bible and the gospels several times in five months. One afternoon, God began to show me pictures in my head of me serving Him in ministry. I saw myself in the pulpit preaching again.

I protested, "No, Lord! You got the wrong guy. There are people that are more faithful, more holy, smarter, more qualified, and much more loyal than I am. I am a failure." Then a verse flooded my mind, "Am I not allowed to do what I choose with what belongs to me?" (Matthew 20:15). I sheepishly agreed that God could do what He wanted with me. I felt the Lord saying that He would heal me of Hepatitis C. He also began to speak to me about a revival that was coming. He said, "I am raising up an army of outcasts out of the prisons and off the streets that will go across this land and preach the unadulterated Gospel of Jesus Christ with signs and wonders following." I vowed to serve the Lord the remainder of my time in prison and for the rest of my life. My prison became a palace. Throughout that five months in the hole the presence of the Lord was tangible. I felt what were like waves of electric liquid love flowing over me. What should have been the worst time in my life was the best!

A correctional facility form. Checkboxes across the top labeled:

- CNMCF/CMRU/CMU — PO Drawer 1328, Los Lunas, NM 87031
- GCCF — P.O. Box 520, Santa Rosa, NM 88435
- LCCF — 6900 W. Millen Dr., Hobbs, NM 88244
- PNM (checked X) — PO Box 1059, Santa Fe, NM 87504
- SNMCF — PO Box 639, Las Cruces, NM 88004
- SNMCF-POU — PO Box 20005, Las Cruces, NM 88004
- WNMCF — PO Drawer 250, Grants, NM 87020

Name: JOHN McHARDIN
No. 67376   Unit: 1B-E-162
Date: 6-16-2008

DAD,

I'm glad you got the father's day card, so Scott seems great &
yes I will be able to work with him. Yesterday, the 13th was
my last day to be in the hole; however, that obviously does not mean
anything. The case worker is new and gives me the run around. The
bottom line is they are lazy or understaffed. Probably a little of both
the report was dropped, the one Bastillos filed against me, for lack of
evidence. I gave Scott a copy of the report. Ask him for a copy meeting...

How are you getting your mail? I noticed the letter was
postmarked & dated June 14th. I will let you know as soon as
I can get visits. I should be off discipline seg. now + able to
get visits. However, it was such an ordeal experience last time that
I am reluctant.

I finished Daniel last nite. So I read all the prophets last week. Today
Ezra + Nehemiah. I had been reading other books (novels etc.) but now I
have no desire. If I listen to talk radio (naughty lol me ve the secular airwaves)
or read secular literature – I immediately feel peace leave. This place
does well (goodbye own). If not for the Lord, I would be lost (on
so many levels.)

According to my journal on 5-29 the Lord spoke to me about.
a revival ushered in by ex-convicts, drug addicts, the foolish things of this
world (i.e. the 'lame'). My notes say, the outpouring will come to the
humble church. Many won't receive it. Like Seymour, the black, half
blind man associated w/ the Azusa Street revival. It was hard for
people to get under him (I know mind you, blacks were subhuman still–at this
time.) God is doing a new thing. Amen.

As I'm writing this I don't feel it will be limited to 'the lame'
but the Lord will use the 'lame' to carry out plunder. I remember
when you sent these verses to me and even 'the lame will carry out
plunder' was underlined. I thought is he saying – I'm lame, or the
audacity... but yes, I am one of the lame-crippled, poor + ineffectual (according to my)
In retrospect it seems quite clear.

67

☐ CNMCF/CMRU/CMU PO Drawer 1328 Los Lunas, NM 87031
☐ GCCF P.O. Box 520 Santa Rosa, NM 88435
☐ LCCF 6900 W. Millen Dr. Hobbs, NM 88244
☐ PNM PO Box 1059 Santa Fe, NM 87504
☐ SNMCF PO Box 639 Las Cruces, NM 88004
☐ SNMCF-POU PO Box 20005 Las Cruces, NM 88004
☒ WNMCF PO Drawer 250 Grants, NM 87020

Name: JOHN CALEB ALARID
No. 67372   Unit 3-103

Date: 9-20-08

Dearest "Poppo",

I just got off the phone w/ you. What would I do w/out you? You are a mentor, friend, co-laborer & a tremendous help in every way. Thanks. :)

Wow. Anaconia + the prison journal in Argentina. A backslidden minister turns back to God + the fire burns + spreads. Brian mentioned it in passing when I asked for prayer for the prisoners. Just before the visit (about 9am) [visit was at 1:30?] I felt the Lord speak the following, I am writing it out for you as per your request. His thoughts flooded my mind faster than I can write:

9-20-08 9am - My cell mate and others say they felt "something" while attending. I said 42&13 ministries at prison chapel. My cellmate said he began shaking + almost passed out. Another guy said that while at Los Lunas Prison (etc.) they came and when she said Jesus, Jesus, Jesus, it thundered 3 times. As I have read Isaiah 42+43 several times + meditated on it. This is what the Lord is speaking to me + I believe to them too." The Lord says,

"Now, I will gather the lame, the outcasts and the things which are not. I will show myself to those who do not seek me. For those who hear my voice I will turn their captivity, darkness will become light before them. I will place my name on them + they will go forth - a mighty & dreadful army. Fire will devour before them, behind them a flame blazes (Joel 2) Like dawn spreading across the mountains, a large & mighty army comes, such as never before. With wonder upon wonder I will astound the religious leaders of your time who hold fast to their traditions + doctrines. Open the gates, sound the alarm, blow the trumpet - here comes the Lord of Glory, the Son of Righteousness cometh w/ healing in His wings. In His right hand is salvation but in His left hand is slaughter. Go tell my prophets the time has come - the former + latter rain in the same month. Behold I am doing a new thing. Now it springs up, do you not perceive it. Before they spring up I announce them to you.

→

At the end of five months I was released from solitary and sent to a facility in Grants, New Mexico. As soon as I got into the unit and was assigned a cell, an old friend came up and said, "Hey Coyote, I got you, Holmes." He allowed me to see a small syringe cuffed in his hand with what appeared to be heroin in it. I went up to him and said. "I don't do that stuff anymore. Don't ever bring that back to me. I have never put a needle in my arm again, or felt a desire for any kind of drug.

I was voted in as inmate pastor and started "420 Prayer Meetings" that went on in all the cell blocks at 4:20 p.m. On the street, "420" meant it was time to get high; however, I switched it to mean 1 Corinthians 4:20, "For the kingdom of God does not consist in talk but in power."

I took undergraduate correspondence courses through the Assemblies of God's Global University and I led the Scared Straight program that dealt with young men who were starting to get into trouble with the law.

After the Lord met me in solitary confinement, the next twenty-seven months in prison were spent with a constant awareness of the presence of God, as if He placed me in a bubble filled with his love and passion. He walked with me and talked with me. Sometimes, doubt would creep in and I would think, "This is not real. I must have done too many drugs." I asked God to reveal to me that this was Him speaking and not the delusions of an ex-addict.

On March 14, 2010, as I walked the yard with other inmates at the state prison in Los Lunas, New Mexico, a severe dust storm came out of nowhere, which is not uncommon in that area. The guards called, "movement," which meant that inmates had ten minutes to move to another area of the facility. After that, the facility would be locked down again. Everyone fled inside because of the dust storm, but I sensed the small, still voice of the Lord say, "Stay out here and walk with me." So, I continued to walk while everyone else went in. The storm subsided shortly after. I felt the beautiful presence of the Lord. He spoke to me as a thought in my mind, but I had a heightened state of awareness. The Lord spoke very clearly: "A 7.2 magnitude earthquake will rock San Diego as a sign that I am speaking to you."

Dearest Dad,   3-M-2010

Greetings. I'm so glad to hear the meetings went well.
Mom came today w/ Chloe + Colin. a It was a nice visit.
I tried to call you this afternoon + evening but could not
get through. Its ok. I'm blessed because you ta are
Speaking + spending time w/ the Saints in His Presence.

This Am as I walked the yard I felt the Lord
say something about a 7.2 earthquake in San Diego.
It would be a sign to me that He will do what
he said he would do.

I'm learning to hear the voice of God. If it does
not happen then I heard wrong + will continue
to wait upon the Lord knowing that He is +
He is a rewarder of those who diligently seek
Him.

Attached is a pamphlet we hand out to
the new inmates at RDC - the NERC class —>
the one I teach across the street.

As I walked the yard this Am - the Lord
kept saying, "I am coming soon." I was getting
frustrated because I have heard those 4 words
many times since Grants. I said Lord what does that
mean + what do you want me to do. He said

Twenty-one days later on April 4, 2010, an earthquake hit
San Diego. It was known as the Easter Earthquake. I did not hear
about it until the morning of April 5, when I woke up and saw
the words on my cellmate's muted television: "A 7.2 Earthquake
Rocks San Diego."

I lay there in shock for several minutes. Then, joy flooded my soul, not because I was happy that an earthquake occurred, but because of God's faithfulness in providing a sign for me. He used His knowledge of the impending earthquake to confirm to me that I was not just making this up. This thing was for real!

My mom and dad came to see me often and my dad kept money on my books. One day when my dad walked into the visiting room I noticed he had on a class ring that looked like my high school ring. That would have been impossible because I had pawned the ring and everything else I owned to get high before I was arrested. Dad said, "This is your high school ring. I went to every pawn shop in Albuquerque until I found it." I cried when he said that. I now wear that ring every day. I'm so grateful for my dad, and my mom. I hurt them and my other loved ones for many years.

In the same way, sometimes we feel like we are hurting God by the bad actions we choose, but He is a good, good Father and He loves us no matter what. My dad never gave up on me. Our God the Father will never give up on us either.

Chapter 6

SET FREE

In May, 2010, I was released from prison after serving less than half of the eight years of my sentence. I was paroled to my father's house in Santa Fe where I attended Christian Life Fellowship church and the local community college. I worked as an English as a Second Language instructor in the school system.

In June, 2010, during church service I walked forward to be prayed for. I wanted my Hepatitis C healed through the prayers of the elders of the church. When I went back to the clinic for the next blood test there was no sign of the virus (HCV). This is a documented healing. The Lord healed me of a disease that I contracted from using dirty needles. He not only forgave my sins, but healed my body. Blessed be the name of the Lord!

Later that year, after I spoke at his service, a pastor told me I should attend Central Bible College (CBC) in Springfield, Missouri. I prayed and felt that the Lord also wanted me to attend CBC. If I had not been healed of HCV, I would have stayed in New Mexico through the end of 2012 for the HCV treatment.

Hannah, my future wife, only attended CBC in 2011. If I did not come when I did I would not have met my beautiful wife, baby Brooklyn would not have been born, and we would not have started Freedom City Church. It is amazing to see how God has guided my life. I know He is guiding yours, too.

While at Central Bible College, I took a team of students out to do street witnessing in downtown Springfield. Tom Moon was one of the students and he, and his wife, Kayla, currently serve as our youth pastors at Freedom City.

I met Tom at a local gym my first month in town. He came up and said, "Hi, do you go to CBC?" I said "yes." We immediately hit it off. I asked if he wanted to pray after we worked out. He said, "Where at?" I said, "In the car with worship music playing." He said "okay." After our workout, I was ready to pray but Tom seemed to be taking a long time to come out and join in. I texted him and said, "Let's just pray another time."

I drove off and thought, "That was a little rude of Tom. If someone is waiting for you to pray, you should hurry."

I went north on Glenstone toward my apartment near the freeway. As I began to drive off, I felt the Lord speak, "Turn around and go back and pray with him."

I argued with God. After all, wasn't I already on my way home? The Lord impressed upon me that if I didn't go back, He would not speak to me anymore. As we obey and walk in the light God gives us, He gives us more. The Lord has only spoken to me that way a few times. I had no choice, or desire, but to obey. I made a U-turn and sent another text to Tom.

My text said, "I am waiting in my car to pray. Come whenever you're ready." In a few minutes he was in the car. We prayed for each other and for revival in Springfield and across the nation. We did this every time we worked out together, several times a week. Tom and his wife, Kayla, are two of the more than thirty Christian brothers and sisters that God has brought into Freedom

City Church, Springfield to form our "Dream Team." Some are pastors with many years of experience and others are recovered addicts with years of hard experience on the streets. All love Jesus. Each contributes his or her unique gifts and talents. Each contributes voluntarily. Only our administrative pastor receives a salary and she does the work of ten people. I also draw a salary, partially augmented by funds from the Freedom City Church Network. When I think of the Dream Team, I am reminded of the people God brought together for the building of the first temple in ancient Jerusalem (Kings 6:1-8:66).

One time as I was taking our team out to street witness, a beautiful Filipina classmate came up to me as we were witnessing outside the Bistro, a local establishment. She asked me if I knew Jesus as my personal Lord and Savior. I said, "Yes. She said, "That's awesome. What do you do?"

I replied, "I go to CBC with you. In fact I sit behind you in AG history." She had no idea. Later this lovely lady, Hannah-Rose, became my wife.

Another time we were street witnessing and we came across a man by the name of Eric. Eric was a huge African-American guy who walked around selling roses. He was hustling money for drugs by handing a rose to a lady, and then asking her date if he would buy the rose for the "pretty lady." Of course, the men needed to show what great guys they were, so they forked money over to Eric. He would make hundreds of dollars in a few hours doing this. The first night we met with him we asked to pray with him. We got in a circle of four Bible school students, me, and Eric. As Tom prayed, Eric began to growl. I knew intuitively that he was demonized. He had a faraway, dazed look in his eyes. I had seen this look and felt this many times in Manilla with oppressed people. My "spidey-senses" were going wild. When Tom finished praying, the man became hostile and came toward me.

I said, "What's your name?" He said, "Satan."

Eric then began to rush me. I cried out. "No, in Jesus name!"

He fell to the ground for a few seconds and then looked up and said, "Who are you guys? Where am I?" He got up and ran off. We worked with Eric for some time, and even started a Bible study at his house. He did okay for a season; however, he returned to drugs. Later, I saw him while ministering at the Greene County jail. He faced fifteen years in prison. I had tried to get him into a Victory Outreach program, but the nearest was in Kansas City. By the time that we got him a ride he changed his mind. This was one of those times when God began to deal with me about opening a church and recovery homes in Springfield.

Healing Testimony

This is a full record of my healing testimony. God moved in powerful ways and brought me to where I am today.

From 1991-1998 and 2003-2007, I was an intravenous heroin addict and drug dealer. In 1998 I met the Lord in a Christian men's home and graduated and later directed the home. During my time as a missionary in Manila, I had an outbreak of jaundice and found out at a hospital that I had Hepatitis C (HCV).

After two years, when I returned to Los Angeles, I was arrested on a fugitive warrant out of Albuquerque. I faced twenty years in prison which depressed me and led me back to my old life of heroin addiction and crime. During that time, my blood became toxic from using too many needles.

I almost died. I spent six months in the hospital with a PICC line of antibiotics going straight into my heart. The doctors also told me that my HCV levels were rising. Still, after being discharged from the hospital, I immediately went back to drugs.

Two years later, in 2006, I was arrested again and sent to prison. In 2008, I had an encounter with Jesus in prison, and my life was changed. In solitary confinement, I read the testimony of an ex-drug addict whose life was transformed. My father sent me pages of this story, and each page was filled with the power of God. This ex-addict was being greatly used by God by laying hands on people and healing them with God's power. I felt the Lord tell me He would heal me, too.

When I was released from solitary and returned to the general population I expected to be immediately healed of the HCV, but I wasn't. However, when I got out of prison in 2010 I found out that the state would pay thirty thousand dollars for my Ribavirin and interferon treatments. This wasn't the best medicine available, but it was all they had. The treatment felt like they were shooting poison into my body, and this would continue for one year. Many people would stay bedridden from side effects for the entire year.

On June 16, 2010, I sat on my dad's deck overlooking the beautiful mountains in Santa Fe. I spent the time reading the Gospel of Luke, chapter 18, verse 41, about a blind beggar crying out for Jesus. The crowds surrounding Jesus told the man to shut up, but he shouted even louder for the Lord's attention. Sometimes desperate situations call for drastic measures.

The Bible tells us how Jesus spoke to the blind man and asked him, "What do you want me to do for you?"

He said, "Lord, let me recover my sight."

I felt the Lord speaking to me gently, "What do you want me to do for you?"

"I want to be healed of HCV," I answered.

The morning of August 4, I met my dad for prayer and Bible study. He said he had been up until 3:00 a.m. that morning in the presence of God, singing, "You are the Lord that healeth me."

On Tuesday, August 10, I traveled in for my last blood work test to be done at St. Vincent's Hospital. I prayed an Old Testament prayer found in the book of Daniel. I told the Lord,

"I know you are able to heal me, but even if you don't, nothing will change between us. I will still serve you with all my heart. I will never bargain with you. I will still preach on divine healing and tell everyone what you are capable of. You hold the words to eternal life. You alone satisfy."

On the way to the hospital the Lord spoke to me from the New Testament book of Romans, "[I am the God] who gives life to the dead and calls into existence the things that do not exist" (Romans 4:17).

I returned to the clinic on August 16 to hear the results of the blood work. The physician's assistant arrived and told me I was healthy enough for the treatments, but the results had yet to come in from my blood work. My heart sank because I didn't feel any different. I didn't think God healed me, but still the physician's assistant wanted to try to do another test. Maybe there was still a chance. I silently sang the song my dad sang over me, "You are the Lord that healeth."

Half an hour later, she came into the little room I waited in and told me there was no trace of HCV in my system. I couldn't believe it, even being a man of faith and believing in God's healing power. I asked for reassurance, and the hospital staff arranged to do another test to confirm. This follow-up test took over a week for results, but the results were incredible, miraculous, and full proof of God's healing."

"Good news", the doctor said, "We are one hundred percent sure there is no virus."

The biblical letter to the Hebrews says that Jesus Christ is the same yesterday, today, and forever! He paid the full price for our spiritual and physical healing on the cross. The Bible says that by his stripes (wounds) we are healed.

This testimony is here to show you that your healing was already paid for over two thousand years ago on the cross of

Calvary. Receive it and accept it! Jesus is alive and well and here to heal you today.

Are any of you sick? I know who you can turn to: Jesus Christ!

Graduation and Fulfillment

In May, 2013, I graduated with a BA in Leadership and Theology. I also married Hannah-Rose, the love of my life. Hannah and her sister were born and raised in Brooklyn, New York, after their parents arrived in the United States from Cebu in the Philippines. She struggled with depression and addiction during her teenage years, but she encountered the Lord at the Teen Challenge program in New York City. She came to CBC in 2011 after she had finished the program.

I am so grateful for my wife, Hannah. She is teaching me to stop and smell the roses in life. I am task and goal oriented. Hannah helps me enjoy the journey. Apart from the Lord Jesus Christ, she is the best thing that has ever happened to me.

After my graduation from CBC, we started attending James River Church in Ozark, Missouri, where we served on the discipleship team and started a "life group" in North Springfield. Because of my fluency in Spanish I got a job as a bilingual faculty member at Global University. I tell people that being half-Mexican finally paid off!

I worked with Rob Weddle, the same guy who used to send undergraduate theological courses to me in prison in New Mexico. I never would have thought when I was completing those courses that I would one day be a faculty member with this guy. It never ceases to amaze me how God connects the dots in our lives. Also at Global were Steven and Linda Long, who were Assemblies of God missionaries in Manila when I was there with Victory Outreach. They were dear friends of our team. Now I was working with them at Global ten years later.

Prison to Pastor

On March 9, 2014, Steve Hill of the Brownsville revival died. His life had a tremendous impact on me. That night as my wife got into bed in our little duplex across from CBC, I looked at her and said, "Who will weep for the lost like Steve Hill did?"

At that moment, I cried with deep moans and tears. I cried for a long time and even fell to the ground in a fetal position. As my wife held me, I wept for the lost in Springfield, and in the nation; not anyone specifically, but the lost across the nation. That's precisely when God placed it in my heart to plant the church and recovery homes in Springfield. I resigned from Global University on May 6, 2015, and we planted Freedom City Church in Springfield and started men's and women's Hope Homes, which are residential discipleship homes that provide freedom and hope to those struggling with life-controlling issues and desperate situations, such as post-incarceration life, addiction, and homelessness. I also serve as an area director for Prison Fellowship ministries.

I enrolled at the Assemblies of God Theological Seminary (AGTS). During my first year there, I met with Steve Pyke, who at the time was the director of the Church Multiplication Network. I told him about my vision to plant churches and recovery homes in Springfield and then across the country based on the Victory Outreach model. He and others encouraged me to move forward with the vision God had given me.

In 2015, I connected with a church planting network out of Pittsburgh to launch our church as CityReach Springfield. We have re-branded as Freedom City Church, the original name God gave me when I was wrote the prospectus for this church-plant years before a class at the Assemblies of God Theological Seminary. Freedom City Movement is the name of our church planting arm. We will plant churches across this country and around the world. Freedom City Church exists to reach those far from God in the urban centers of the world with the message and hope of Jesus Christ in order to grow together as committed Christ-followers.

Since my arrival in Springfield, I have been going weekly to local jails and prisons to preach the Gospel. Last year, more than three hundred men professed faith in Christ at our altar calls. For his glory, the Lord is using my past pain and failures to bring hope to other addicts and convicts.

Many inmates encounter God and serve Jesus in prison; however, they fall away when they are released back into society. There are many obstacles released offenders face. It is our job as the church, to embrace and disciple these men and women. It is not enough to minister at the prison or evangelize in the neighborhoods. We must do the hard, frustrating, and time-consuming work of discipleship. This is the New Testament pattern. Hannah and I are both products of residential Christ-centered recovery programs.

The released prisoners need a controlled environment where they can learn to live out their faith, and a community of Christ-followers that will share God's love. The Hope Homes are much like incubators for premature babies. The homes are also boot camps where future world changers are trained and equipped. The Lord spoke to me in prison many years ago about an army that He will raise up out of prisons and off the streets to go across this land to preach the unadulterated Gospel of Jesus Christ with great boldness and power. We are humbled to be part of that movement.

"Hardships often prepare ordinary people
for an extraordinary destiny." –C. S. Lewis

I am grateful for my wife, Hannah. She is truly a gift from God in my life. She has taught me to laugh again. She is my closest friend, and the most sincere Christ-follower I know.

John and Hannah the day before they were married in 2013.

John and Hannah with John's mother Carla, his brother and sister-in-law Brian and Mercy, and nieces and nephews Chloe, Colin, and Lauren.

I am also grateful for my father, mother, and brother. I believe I am still alive today and on fire for God in answer to their prayers.

My wife, our team, and I are excited to see what the Lord is doing next through Freedom City Church and our Hope Homes. I serve as lead pastor and church planter, and my wife, Hannah, is the worship pastor. We launched Freedom City Church in Springfield on March 6, 2016. In the first month, more than twenty people surrendered their lives to Christ. The Hope Home for men opened on April 1, 2016, and the women's home opened in January, 2017. In fall, 2017, we are launching five churches in the Midwest and three in Missouri. God is on the move.

In May, 2016, I graduated with a Master of Arts from AGTS. Dr. Mark Hausfeld, seminary president, honored me by asking me to be a class speaker. Then he asked if I would be willing to wear an orange prison jumpsuit to give my speech. Years ago, while in solitary confinement at the state prison in Santa Fe, I had a dream that I was on a stage with many distinguished people; however, I had on an orange prison jumpsuit. Intuitively I knew some people were looking at me and saying, "How did that guy get up there with all those important people?" This was a literal fulfillment of that dream! All glory to God for the great things He has done for his servant.

John and his father, Robert Alarid, at his graduation from Central Bible College in 2013.

John preaching at the church building on Broadway.

A few years ago the Lord impressed upon me that He would give us the church building on 1477 North Broadway Avenue. My wife and I stood on this word and we prayed over the building, Jericho marched around it, and did prayer circles with friends. I even put a picture up in my office of the property with a banner pen that said "CityReach, Springfield" so I could pray and be reminded of the promise of God. When God gives a promise begin to visualize it and pray for it, even though the promise may be delayed.

Always remember that God's timing is perfect, not ours. God will always keep his word. Through a series of miracles the Lord opened the church door to us, and in January, 2017, I walked into Hogan Land Title Company. With no money down, I signed a paper and walked out with the keys to our new property. We now own a twenty-five thousand square foot property in the heart of North Springfield. We launched services in our new building on Mother's Day, May 14, 2017. On July 16 we held the first graduation for our nine-month men's Hope Home program.

I am a keynote speaker for Prison Fellowship ministries. In July, 2017, I went to speak at a prison in Omaha with the governor of Nebraska and the CEO of Prison Fellowship in attendance. Prison Fellowship pays all expenses and gives me an honorarium. Who would have thought that one day I would get paid to go to prisons to speak? I, who was so drugged up at one point in my life that almost no one could understand me. Only God could orchestrate something like this. I speak regularly at prison revivals. I can testify that God is raising up that army of outcasts, prodigals, ex-cons, and ex-junkies that will go across this land and preach the unadulterated Gospel of Jesus Christ with signs and wonders following. I believe the greatest hours of the church are right in front of us. This is the time to take back our cities for the honor and glory of Jesus Christ!

Afterword

Every Sunday morning and Friday night people respond to the altar calls to surrender their lives to Jesus. Following Steve Hill's pattern, I call people to repent and turn to God. Many have shared that they have felt the tangible presence of God in the services. Many tears of repentance are shed. Over the past few years, thousands have surrendered their lives to Christ at our local church and in the local prisons and jails. We are experiencing what I believe to be a mighty move of God.

The best is yet to come! Join the movement wherever you are!

> He raises up the poor from the dust; he lifts the needy from the ash heap to make them sit with princes and inherit a seal of honor. For the pillars of the earth are the LORD'S, and on them he has set the world. (1 Samuel 2:8)

> And they have conquered him by the blood of the Lamb and by the word of their testimony, for they loved not their lives even unto death. (Revelation 12:11)

By His Grace,

John Caleb Alarid

Lead Pastor | Freedom City Church - Springfield, MO
Executive Director | Hope Homes of the Ozarks
Area Director | Prison Fellowship Ministries
email: johna@freedomcitychurch.org

Testimonies of God's Freeing Grace

Jason

After fighting the biggest RICO death penalty case in U.S. history, the Holy Spirit finally, through Pastor John's ministry (among others), delivered me from studying terrorism (chemistry, explosives, poisons, drugs, and more), raised me from the dead, and set me free to reflect the radical LOVE of CHRIST JESUS. Pastor John trusts me, an ex-psychopath, as a friend and leader in his church, and as manager of the Hope Home of the Ozarks.

The world says psychopaths can't change, but JESUS said that HE is the resurrection and the life. Prison couldn't change my codefendants or me, so the prosecutors spent over 200 million dollars trying to kill us. Then JESUS did what man couldn't do: HE raised me from the dead for free; zero cost to taxpayers!

I had been an outlaw. That's all I ever wanted to be. That's really all the life I ever knew. My family members were all outlaws. I saw my dad killed right in front of me on my fourteenth birthday. My mother was shot on the day of the funeral. Only days later, my granddad was killed.

One time, after my release from prison, one of my outlaw buddies got burned up cooking drugs and I went to his funeral. When I walked into the service the PA system was playing a song about Jesus. The lyrics were something like, "The more I seek You, the more I find You, the more I find You, the more I love You." Later I found out it was by a singer and songwriter named Kari Jobe. As I heard the song, I started crying. I knew the tears were not for my buddy. I knew the Lord had got me good! I had never felt such love. Suddenly I was addicted to that powerful love!

I joined Harvest Assembly in Oak Grove, Arkansas, and began to be involved with the evangelism team. We were up in Springfield one day and I heard about Pastor Alarid and Freedom City Church. They were just beginning and I thought how great it would be to go to that church and work with a pastor like John Alarid, someone who would not look at me differently because of my background. He was someone who had been to prison, too. I knew a little bit about prisons, having done twenty-one years on a ten-year sentence!

I had worked for two years with the Presbytery in Arkansas, but they had shut down their recovery home. I got to meet Pastor John through one of the Arkansas pastors. My desire became reality and here I am.

David

In 2014, strung out on heroin, on the run from a lifetime of addiction and crime, and broken from a series of tragic circumstances, I found myself homeless and living under a bridge in Portland, Oregon.

I remember waking up one morning under the Broadway Bridge on my bed, a piece of cardboard box I had dug out of a dumpster. I was dope sick, throwing up green bile, my feet were blistered, and I was in a state of despair. I cried out to God to save me from this place that seemed to resemble hell on earth. About a week later, God showed up in the form of extradition services (Con Link). I was brought back to Greene County jail in Springfield on felony charges. I was suffering from withdrawals, more mental than physical at this point, mainly anxiety and depression.

I decided to get a break from my pod by attending a chapel service. When I got to the chapel, I sat down with my orange sandals and striped uniform. Pastor John spoke and I began to listen to his testimony. His testimony, in my mind, was so similar to where I had just been that I fully connected emotionally. Pastor John related how he overcame a life of crime and addiction by a personal relationship with Jesus Christ. He spoke about being in solitary confinement in Santa Fe, New Mexico, when God showed up, poured out his overwhelming love, washed away John's sin, and made him new.

John began to receive visions of men and women being raised up out of prisons across the nation. They were being raised up to preach the unadulterated gospel of Jesus Christ with great boldness and power with signs and wonders following. I also remember him talking about opening a church in Springfield that would be passionate about reaching the lost. I answered the altar call that day and gave my life to Jesus. I was filled with hope and encouragement for a brighter future.

For me, however, it wasn't "Abracadabra, you're saved and set free." It was definitely, and still is, a process. I went on to prison for a few months, was released, and soon relapsed, returning to the same old life I thought I had left. I had no support, structure, or accountability. Most of all I knew there was something missing: I just didn't know what that was.

I soon found myself lying on a cement floor on top of a busted green mat, dope sick, and locked up in a physical and mental cell. I began to weep tears of anguish from deep within my soul. I cried out to God and begged Him to reveal what it was that I was missing. I began to ask God to take control of my life, not only spiritually, but physically. Given my circumstances, that meant legally as well.

I was soon sentenced to one year at Ozark Correction Center in Fordland, Missouri. I began to read the Bible every day and to attend every church service I possibly could. God gave me greater and greater revelation of who Jesus Christ really is, and I believe that in that time of anguish when I was crying out to God is when He sent the power of the Holy Spirit to fill me with a passion to go after Christ with all my heart.

About a month into my stay at OCC, I was attending a chapel service that was being conducted by a church called Freedom City Church, Springfield. Pastor John was there now sharing about how he had graduated from the Assemblies of God Theological Seminary with a masters degree. Instantly, I was captivated and drawn to remembrance of a few years back when I gave my life to Christ in the Greene County jail. Pastor John had planted his church, Freedom City Church, in North Springfield. He said Hope Homes were now open for men and women who were sold out for Jesus Christ.

I was baptized by Freedom City Church a few months later and I did my interview for the program and was released from OCC in April, 2017. The Hope Home allowed me to establish myself in a body of believers who held me accountable and who believed in me and supported me through all my struggles.

Before the Hope Home, I had been in and out of prison six times and had used every time within a few days of being released. On Thanksgiving, 2018, I will have three years clean from drugs and over two years with no cigarettes. I just finished my second semester of community college and I start Bible college in fall, 2018, for a bachelor's degree in biblical studies. God gave me what I was missing: Godly support and accountability. I proclaim victory over the lies of the enemy and I attest to the vision of an army of blood bought, word taught front line soldiers who will take back everything the enemy ever stole for the honor and glory of Jesus Christ.

Timothy

From Dope Addict to Hope Addict! I have known Jesus Christ my entire life but there was a season that I walked away from Him. Here is my story.

I grew up in a very devoted Pentecostal family with strong Christian values that went to church at least four times a week. But, as I grew older into my teenage years, I started to go away from it. By the time I was sixteen, I had quit going to church altogether except for special occasions. At this point in my life, I had met a woman who was a few years older than I. We started a relationship and before long she became pregnant. We were married by the time I was seventeen, in 1982.

On August 4, 1982, I was blessed with the birth of my son. I was the happiest person alive, but my happiness was soon to change. On October 23, 1982, I walked up to my son's room to get him for his grandfather who had come for dinner. When I went into his room, I found my son dead in his crib. The paramedics tried unsuccessfully to resuscitate him and a few days later we buried the best part of me.

I remember I was so broken and angry with God! I was empty and bitter and believed that the God that I grew up knowing was responsible for my son's death and that as long as I lived I would never trust in Him again. I vowed that I was never again going to feel the way I did the day my son died.

So began my long multi-decade journey into a self-induced hell that would become my life. I began to drink heavily and smoke more weed and work as much as I could; anything I could do to keep my mind busy and my emotions dead. My marriage began to deteriorate. My wife needed someone to talk to about what had happened with our son and I wasn't going to be the one. I completely shut down about it as if I never even had a son. By 1987, our marriage was over.

I took a job working on the road removing asbestos. The money was good and the drugs were easy to get. By this time, I had already begun using cocaine and methamphetamine intravenously. In 1990, I had my first cocaine overdose. I had developed a habit that consisted of over an eightball every day and a half, all the while consuming massive amounts of alcohol and various other drugs including speed, acid, and mushrooms. At the same time, I was working full-time sixty to eighty hours a week. From 1982 to 2010, I overdosed three times and had seven or eight wrecks in which I should have been severely injured, but unbeknownst to me, God had his hand on my life.

In 1992, I remarried, but all that time I tried to maintain my drug use without my wife's knowledge. That marriage actually lasted for approximately twenty-two years before I was served divorce papers in jail.

In 2010, the same year my wife divorced me, I was terminated from my job as senior project superintendent for the asbestos company. This happened while I was off after having carpal tunnel surgery on both hands. Without any way to support myself or my drug habit, I became a dealer.

In 2012, God had finally had enough of my running from Him and on December 21, He blessed me with a federal grand jury indictment for distribution of methamphetamines. But, I continued to run and do drugs for the next ten months or so. Finally, on November 14, 2013, I turned myself in to start serving my time.

I had wrecked or ruined every relationship I ever had over the course of this thirty-one year period. I was spiritually broken and destitute. My life had no meaning. My word had no value, and my walk had no purpose. I literally did not care if I lived or died. I was a hopeless drug addict. Yet, God wasn't through with me.

I had been in Greene County jail for about two weeks and my head had finally started clearing up. I began to worry about what I was facing time-wise. Up until then I hadn't put together two sober days to think in over thirty-one years. One night, I went to sleep and while I was asleep I had a vivid dream. In that dream, I was standing in front of that little old Pentecostal church I had grown up in, but in my dream I was a grown man. The church had a concrete porch with a set of stairs on each side going up to the doorway. In that doorway stood a man by the name of W.B. McCarthy, my old minister from my childhood. At the time of my dream, he had been dead some twenty-five or thirty years. But, there he was and he was standing up there with his arms stretched out and he said these four words, "Why haven't you called?"

I remember running up the right side of the stairs and collapsing into his arms and weeping uncontrollably. I cried, "I'm sorry, I'm sorry, I'm sorry!" The love and the warmth coming off of him permeated my entire body. I don't know how long I was asleep after that, but when I woke up I was still crying. I had this Bible verse in my head from my distant childhood: Deuteronomy 31:6. The verse is, "Be strong and of a good courage, fear not, nor be afraid of them: for the Lord thy God, he it is that doth go with thee; he will not fail thee, nor forsake thee."

At that point, I knew that the same Jesus I had met when I was a six-or-seven-year-old kid in that little church had been with me my entire life, even in the darkest times when I did not want Him there. He had come to me in a dream with a familiar face at a familiar place so that for me there was no mistaking who

He was. I knew in my heart that if I turned my life back over to Him, He would do some amazing things with me.

The very next chapel service at the jail that I attended there was a man who preached by the name of John Alarid. He was preaching the same message with the same determination as my old minister, and I knew that God had set up this divine encounter. After the sermon, Pastor John gave an altar call and I rededicated my life to Jesus. I did not know at the time what kind of an impact that God had planned for Pastor John to make upon my life. For the next five months, I saw Pastor John once a month. Then I was sent to federal prison. I didn't give John too much thought after I left because he had said that he was going back to the west coast and New Mexico to start his ministry and outreaches. The entire time I was in federal I stood on the verse and promise that God had given me in my dream. I was blessed the whole time! I met some really good Christian brothers in prison and we all grew closer to the Lord.

I was released to the federal halfway house in Springfield in April, 2015, and began looking for a church I could call home. I could never find one that fit; never one I felt I belonged in. In March, 2016, I was sitting at my sister's house looking through my phone and I came across this newspaper article that read, "New Church in Springfield Wants to Make a Difference." I thought to myself, "they all say that, but few do." I went ahead and started scrolling through the article. When I got to the bottom of the page there was a photo of Pastor John and his wife, Hannah. I literally felt my heart jump and I told my sister I had to go see this man! The very next Sunday I walked into the church meeting and I could see Pastor John across the room. I walked up to him and said, "Man, the last time I saw you I was in county jail." That was the third week of the launch of Freedom City Church Springfield.

When I walked into that building I knew that this lost sheep had found his flock, and that God had called me to this church. I am now a deacon and am studying for my ministry certification. I will one day follow in my father's footsteps as a preacher, fulfilling the prophecy that my mother spoke of me as a small child in that little Pentecostal church so many years ago.

Allan

I grew up in Lawton, Oklahoma, in a family of four with my brother, father, and mother. We had no major family traumas or issues. I did not drink in high school but became a binge drinker when I went off to the University of Oklahoma and joined a fraternity.

I married my college sweetheart, Betty, and we headed to New York City for me to find my fortune in advertising. I became a media buyer at a major New York advertising agency and, as such, controlled placement of hundreds of thousands of dollars of Clairol advertising. Buyers in my position were heavily wined and dined by magazine and broadcast sales representatives. As time went on, I realized that the big incomes were earned by the sales reps so I transferred to broadcast sales. I became the "winer and diner." The three-martini lunch was quite popular in those days and I had an unlimited expense account.

My company transferred me to Philadelphia as their regional sales manager. The pace slowed somewhat but the entertaining didn't. I then decided to go be a general sales manager for an AM and FM combination radio station in Pittsburgh, Pennsylvania. More drinking and entertaining! But, my drinking caught up with me in Pittsburgh and I was fired. My life had become "unmanageable" as it says in step one of Alcoholics Anonymous. The only problem was that I didn't realize that was the problem, so I kept on drinking. The broadcast business being what it is,

I landed on my feet in St. Louis with a higher salary and bigger title as general manager of the Doubleday Broadcasting AM and FM radio stations.

The broadcast business also being what it is, Doubleday decided to divest of its broadcasting properties. Out of work again! I then chose to purchase a one-third interest in KGBX-AM radio in Springfield. I put together some investors and became president of the corporation and general manager of the radio station. Betty was a begrudging partner because she was not eager to be involved in such a large investment. My continued drinking, poor business decisions, and general inability to run a profitable operation forced us into a situation where we had to auction the station at a great loss. Counting all the investors, we lost hundreds of thousands of dollars. Betty and I lost our life savings and our home. I personally hit rock bottom, was suicidal, and had given up all hope.

Then God stepped in and engineered the circumstances which led to my meeting with a former drinking buddy of my dad's, Bob Parr. Bob had been a member of A.A. for many years and was also a Methodist lay preacher. We met at my mother's house in Enid, Oklahoma. As Bob was telling me his story of how he became sober, all of my pain and anguish flew out of my chest as through a great hole and was replaced by a profound sense of peace flowing in through my back. I knew in my heart that everything was going to be all right. I had never had any knowledge or experience that God was real, but from that point on I knew without a doubt.

I no longer had any desire for alcohol; the compulsion that had dominated my life for more than thirty years was completely gone. The Holy Spirit led me to John, chapters 14-16 which totally explained what was going on in my life. Through no effort of my own, God had reached down, saved me, and filled me with his wonderful Spirit! Soon, I also quit smoking, cursing, writing hot checks, lying, and gambling (I loved to gamble). I didn't miss those vices at all: I felt freed from the terrible bondages.

The Holy Spirit led me to used book stores and guided me to certain books, primarily in the religion sections. I began to feel that I was supposed to attend seminary which, given my background as a secular, slobbering drunk, was almost laughable. But, I wound up enrolling at the Assemblies of God Theological Seminary, which was a huge leap coming from my limited church experience in a mainline denomination.

By the time I enrolled at AGTS, the Holy Spirit had basically given me a Bible school education through the used books. I experienced the supernatural at AGTS and developed a yearning to be in the presence of God—there is no greater feeling! I graduated with a Master of Divinity in 2000 and became a preacher. The Holy Spirit had also led me into jail and prison ministry.

One day I received a phone call from a professor at Central Bible College asking if I would talk to one of his students who was interested in getting into jail and prison ministry. The student was John Alarid. We met and he filled out his application to be a volunteer at the Greene County jail. The officer in charge of volunteers told me he thought John, given his background, had no real chance of being approved. Of course, John was miraculously approved and the rest is history.

I heard John's visions for his church and Hope Homes as we ministered. There was no doubt in my mind that I wanted to be part of this great work of God! It has been marvelous to be on this wild and wonderful ride witnessing God's miracles through changed and saved lives!

Bailey

On April 26 of this year [2018] I found myself sitting on the bathroom floor ready to end it all. My life was out of control and I needed the downward spiral to stop. After five years of heavy heroin use, I had lost everything I had ever dreamed of—my family's trust, my education, a job that I enjoyed, the love of my life, and the one thing I'm most proud of, my precious little boy, Bentley.

I didn't have the addiction—the addiction had me. I was on a fast track to destruction and death and heroin was in the driver's seat. By the grace of God, even after I attempted to end it all, I woke up hours later, still on the bathroom floor, still in my miserable state of being, and already with the desperate need to find my next fix.

Less than 24 hours later I found myself locked up in a jail cell. As surprising as this unexpected turn of events was to me, I now know that the unexpected is never unexpected to God. God knew that day would come in my life and He was already in that day waiting for me, even in that jail cell. He met me there, and he loved me there in the lowest point of my life. What I did not know at that time was that my parents had prayed that very difficult prayer: do whatever it takes, God, to save her life.

Two weeks prior to my arrest, Pastor John Alarid and some of the Hope Homes' residents had visited my church in my small hometown of Salem, Missouri. My mom and my cousin felt led to ask Pastor John and the Hope Homes' group to pray for me. I believe as a result that my arrest was God's intervention to rescue me from the darkness that was destroying me.

After I was finally released from jail, I came to the Hope Home and am now celebrating over sixty days of hope. I may have scars on my arms, but I have Jesus in my heart and He has given me the victory. I am a new creation in Christ and here at the Hope Home I have the opportunity to reflect, pray, grow, and learn to see myself as God sees me. I am learning to love myself again. I am choosing not to be defined by my past. I will not let addiction set the tone for my future, derail my destiny, or stop me from living every moment God has for me. Although the devil had plans to destroy me, he failed, and I am coming back stronger than ever before because I am not alone! I believe God planted me here with a purpose, and I will keep living, loving, and seeking after the One who made me, the One who kept me, and the One who loves me like no other.

David and Susan

David: Although we have not struggled with the type of addictions typical to this church's demographic, we feel a tremendous attraction to the central mission of Freedom City Church (formerly CityReach Church). I am a retired Evangel professor and I teach Growth Track and plan special events for the church. Susan is an adjunct professor at Evangel and heads up women's ministries for the church. We believe that this church's mission falls under the original project of Jesus Christ Himself: reaching out to the one who seems farthest away.

It is the sick who need a physician. That project is the most difficult and requires the most sacrifice to accomplish. To disciple and form believers, not simply inform them, is the heart of the Master. We've watched many great Christians come and go because of the level of difficulty inherent in this grass roots ministry. It's not for the faint of heart and that's why the Smiths are here and plan to persevere!

Susan: My husband, David, and I have been professors at Evangel University (David as Theater Director and I as vocal music professor) since 1980. We have both retired, but still teach and consult as adjuncts. Pastor John's wife, Hannah, was my voice student and she had asked on a few occasions to reschedule her lessons to attend church planting seminars with her husband because they were in the process of planting a church.

We became Facebook friends and I read one of Hannah's posts that described her struggles. I had no idea that this beautiful, godly young woman had a past involving depression and addiction. I recognized some of Hannah's hurts and struggles as some of the same hurts and struggles that our own son had experienced. Without telling John and Hannah about my son, I invited them to dinner. Our son was sick that night and couldn't come, but we heard John's testimony and his passion to reach the lost. We invited them again the next week. The minute that our son walked into the room he and John experienced an instant bond!

At that time, our son had been experiencing severe night terrors and actual demonic attacks. Pastor John told us that he had some of the same experiences in the past. He asked us to pray and fast with him and bring our son to Friday Night Fire. We did. Pastor John prayed with us and God immediately delivered our son from night terrors and the demonic attacks. That night our son also met the lovely young woman (the church Children's Director) who is now his wife and our beloved daughter-in-law.

Pastor John asked us if we would consider becoming elders in the church and we said, "Yes!" He said, "Don't you want to pray about it?" We said, "We already have!" Since then, David has become a Community Care Pastor and I have become the Women's Ministries Pastor. Our son, who had been without work for two and a half years, now has a wonderful job and a beautiful Christian wife. They have bought a house and have given us a precious granddaughter.

We believe in what Freedom City Church is doing because we have experienced it firsthand!

Heather

I started using meth when I was seventeen. I got clean so many different times, but never stayed clean. I got clean in 2009 after I rolled my truck. I flew out, hit a tree, and landed on a barbed wire fence. My truck rolled side to side then end over end. When it stopped it had landed on top of me. By the grace of God, and thinking of my son Seth who was five at the time, I lived.

After a short jail stay and a visit from my parents, I got out and got clean. I was clean for five years. I was doing everything right when I relapsed in 2014. I let my addiction take over. My parents kicked me out and kept my kids. In the four years since then I have been in three different abusive relationships. I have been homeless and running the streets. I have been beaten and pistol-whipped by an ex. I have been raped, robbed at gun point, and pistol-whipped again. An ex has shot at me numerous times. I have tried to hang myself twice.

In June, 2017, I was beaten up once again and told to leave where I was staying. I walked down Broadway and collapsed in front of Freedom City Church church where the men and women of the Hope Homes stopped and prayed for me and asked me to come into the women's home. I said "No, I just need a ride." I wasn't ready to quit my addiction! I ended up back with my ex. He went to jail in July. I was hustling and wound up in jail in August. I spent five months of twelve in the Greene County jail.

The first time I ever heard of Pastor John's book, *My Prison Became a Palace*, was during one of my times in Greene County jail. When I started reading it there were only two copies in the pod. There was a line for the book and girls were arguing about who got the book next. By the time I left there were seven copies in the pod.

Now, looking back, I know it was God who led me to Pastor John's book. It made me stop and look at my own life. Being an addict from a young age, I have always heard many tragic stories of peoples' lives. I never heard a success story until I read Pastor John's book. His book outlines everything we go through as addicts. It made me stop and really think about my life, and how God kept encountering me, but every time I would go back to my old ways. It took me two days to read the book and I realized that God had always been directing my life and had a plan for me. He would turn the bad things into good. God kept putting people in my life who would try to get me to come to church and draw closer to Him. But, my stubborn self wouldn't listen until He put me in jail where I could read Pastor John's book.

I applied for the Hope Home, and was accepted. Then I was released from jail to the program. God knew I needed a success story to change my life. Pastor John's book literally saved my life. It also has given me the strength to be able to share my own testimony.

I was released April 9, 2018, into the Hope Home. I reported to court April 10. My parole officer was not happy with my decision to go to the Hope Home. She didn't believe in a "Christian" program and would not even talk to Pastor John on the phone. We went back to court on April 13 with Pastor John and the judge allowed me to stay in the program.

The year before when I said "No," God had his plan. He knew where I belonged and He patiently led me. He is teaching me to keep my mouth shut when something makes me angry and is helping me to understand that "street respect" and "street mentality" don't matter in his world. It only leads to flophouses, being robbed and beaten, doing everything wrong, and winding up in jail. God is showing and teaching me how He wants me to live. I have been clean for eleven months and my family is back in my life, even my sister who has recently stopped using.

My family has been coming to church. I am working on my relationships with them all. My boys are showing me more love and support than ever. God has even changed my PO's mind. She sees that this program is really helping me. Thanks to God, Pastor John, Ginny my Home Director, all my brothers and sisters in the Hope Homes, and all my Freedom City Church family, I am learning to live a better life through Jesus Christ. God is molding me into the Godly woman He wants me to be!

Marvin

I was born in St. Louis, Missouri, and was raised by my grandmother and mother. I have one sister and three brothers. We were raised up going to church and having Bible studies at home.

I was a rebellious child at fifteen. I left home and got with a notorious gang in St. Louis called the 6 Deuce Crips. I got into a lot of gang violence, drug sales, and prison. On August 25, 2015, I was picked up for a parole violation and possession of a controlled substance. I was a repeat offender so I was in a situation where I could do the rest of my life in prison depending on if the judge thought I was not fit to return to society with a background like mine. The parole board and judge had grace on me and gave me another chance.

I knew it was time to change my way of life, and my way of thinking. So I came to the Hope Home on February 1, 2018. I had my first real encounter with Christ after I heard Pastor John speak. I felt our stories were so much alike. I gave my life back to

God thanks to the Father, Son, and Holy Ghost, and Pastor John and the church.

Shelly

I was born into a Christian home. My dad was a preacher and I accepted Jesus as my savior when I was eight. I knew I was saved, but I hadn't developed a real relationship with God yet.

My parents had a lot of marital problems and argued a lot. When I was twelve I decided I was going to rebel and I turned to the world for comfort. I started experimenting with drugs and as a teen tried meth for the first time.

I got married when I was nineteen. My husband and I were both partiers and spent much of our time getting high. Six months after getting married I became pregnant with my daughter. I was four months pregnant before I found out and felt horrible because I was using and didn't know I was pregnant. I stopped using and prayed for God to forgive me and not take my sin out on my child. God was faithful to answer my prayers!

A year later I had my son and began raising my children in the nurture and admonition of the Lord. But then tragedy struck. My brother committed suicide and bad things just kept happening. My husband left us and I remarried someone who turned out to be abusive and I started drinking to cope. We got away from him, but things got worse inside me. My doctor put me on a bunch of pills which didn't help and eventually I went back to meth. This time it took me to the bottom. For the next five to six years, I was hopelessly addicted and away from my family. It was the worst time of my life. I thought I had no hope.

However, my parents and children were praying for me and God began to get ahold of my heart! One day I cried out to Him,

"God, I don't know how my life got this bad, but will you please help me?"

Again, He was faithful! Not long after that I went to Teen Challenge where He completely restored my life and my family and healed me of all my past! He forgave me and made me new! I learned who God really is and how to depend on Him and trust Him and now all I want to do is serve Him.

When I came home from treatment I had a hard time finding a church that felt like home. I said to God, "I need to be around people like me," and He supernaturally led me to Freedom City Church! He gave me a church full of people like me and even a pastor like me! I'm so thankful for Pastor John and his story and his heart to reach those who are still lost and suffering in addiction. Freedom City Church is my home!

David and Terri

Why are we at Freedom City Church on the north side of Springfield? We live about five minutes away from the mega church we were volunteer ministry partners in for nearly twenty years. We now drive thirty minutes to join Pastor John Alarid in reaching "the one" lost in sin, addiction, despair, hopelessness, and tragedy with the redeeming message of Jesus Christ, the Savior of the world.

How did we get here? Terri and I have a heart for the marginalized and lost of society. We know God can redeem the lowest, lost sinner to a place at the King's table. "He is our peace who has broken down every wall . . ."

We had previously met Pastor John and his wife, Hannah, at our former church. Terri was working in prison ministry when Pastor John spoke at the Federal Medical Center. I had my eye on the launch of Freedom City Church and was following it on social media. Together, we decided it was time for a visit. We've never looked back! As Terri states, "John Alarid is an exceptional follower of Christ. He is chosen, called, committed, and unwavering in his quest to accomplish God's mandate for his life. This love debt is his single focus to 'reach the one farthest away in sin' in abandonment. His fearless, ferocious approach to that goal will stimulate any heart of faith to make the gift of time a priority for Kingdom purposes."

Yes, amazing things are happening at Freedom City Church! Every service is purposely planned to reach the lost and hurting. From early service prayer, to worship, to personal testimony time, to preaching, and to the altar call invitation, the people respond to the Lord's call: "Come and follow me . . ."

Every service has respondents answering His call. It's what church should be and what Freedom City Church is!

Kyle

Our God is a God of miracles and can do more than I can ask for or could ever imagine. For ten years I was a hopeless heroin addict and struggled with the deep, dark cycle of addiction. I experienced homelessness for some time and would sleep next to dumpsters on top of pizza boxes. I was surrounded by the smell of filth and shame. There seemed to be no hope for me. Now thirty, I spent the majority of my twenties in rehabs, jails, and prisons. I would always return back to the same old life.

In 2016, after being on the run for over a year with felony warrants, I was arrested one late summer night. The local police department arrived six cars deep on my front lawn to arrest me. Tired of running I went outside, stated my name and that I had felony warrants for my arrest. That night I gave up from running any longer. I hit my knees and threw my hands into the air. Little did I know then, but that very night I surrendered my life back over to the Lord as he was calling me back home.

Shortly thereafter, I was shipped to prison and while I was there the Lord began his work in me. I poured into prayer and his Word. I was sharing my story one day with a fellow brother and he told me that there was this pastor in Springfield named John Alarid. He stated that Pastor John's church had intense discipleship homes and guys were being set free from addictions and being transformed there! As soon as I heard this, I wanted to know more. I decided to seek out faith-based programs and find out all I could about them.

Walls began to be thrown up blocking me from being accepted to all the other programs except for the men's Hope Home which was one of Pastor John's church's homes. Then God spoke to me: "Trust me." God told me that the Hope Home in Pastor John's Freedom City Church was where my family would be. God told me that's where he wanted me to be with the family I had been praying for.

One day, from prison, I called the number I had found for the Hope Home. Amazingly, Pastor John answered. He told me that he only had a few minutes to talk because he was in New York stepping off the Staten Island Ferry headed to a conference about opening up some more Hope Homes. Right then I had a God-given thought, "That could be me in five years, in New York stepping off the Staten Island Ferry to raise some Hope Homes." Pastor John asked me about my story then prayed for me and accepted me. The summer of 2017, through God's grace, I entered the men's Hope Home.

Not even two months later God fulfilled his promise of that thought he gave me and I found myself in New York stepping off the Staten Island Ferry! God is so good! I wasn't raising up Hope Homes yet, but I was raising money for the homes by working at an event. I was in awe of how amazing God is!

While in New York I would have complete strangers come up to me and say, "I just see Jesus all over you; you are glowing with his love," and then they would smile and walk away. God continued to reveal himself to me the whole time. That trip changed my life.

Since I've been at Freedom City Church, and after hearing Pastor John's story first-hand, my life has continued to be changed and transformed through God's mercy and grace. I've never felt more at home with such a big, loving family. Pastor John is one of us and has been through everything I've been through. He's come out of the darkness and into the light through our Lord. His testimony made me realize there is hope for all that are lost. Pastor John has been such a huge inspiration in my life and he always keeps it real. He keeps it one hundred per cent! I love that about him, and he has such a huge heart and sees the best in people.

What God has done in both our lives is a true miracle. I'm forever grateful for God finding me and leading me to where I am today.

Jamie

I was born into a loving family. My mom and dad were married and always present in my life. We weren't wealthy by any means, but I never wanted for anything. I honestly couldn't have asked for a better family. There was just one thing: my parents drank and smoked weed all the time. I was so loved that I felt like I had to protect them by covering up what they did because of the stigma of people, especially parents, who use. It became a burden that I was unaware I was carrying.

None of that really affected me outwardly at first, I thought. At first I just saw it as normal, but it did affect me. I began smoking weed at age 12 with my older boyfriend. By age 14 what I thought was my happy life took a turn for the worse. I had been smoking weed off and on for a while at this point. This was the year that I found out that my mom had stage 4 lung cancer. I remember staying out late at night because the screams coming from her room were unbearable for me as a young girl. The radiation she was receiving was burning her skin and causing her a lot of pain. These late nights out with my wild older boyfriend led to me losing my virginity, and shortly after that I lost my mom.

I grew up quickly. Mom's pain and death caused my dad to isolate and turn to drugs and alcohol more than ever. I was so alone, confused, and lost. We began to pay the bills with my mom's life insurance check. I felt like that money was my only chance at having a future and it was dwindling fast.

By age 16, I was snorting meth before school and doing OxyContin after. I became very depressed, but despite my growing fears, loneliness, and depression I graduated high school with honors. I went on to college and at age 21 I had my beautiful son, Makson. Up until that point, Makson was the only really good thing that happened to me and he was wonderful.

Life went well for once, but as a dog returns to its vomit I returned to drugs: this time with a needle. My son's dad and I were addicted to opiates and in 2013 I found myself all at once with a baby to raise by myself. I had watched my son's dad on the evening news: he had robbed a pharmacy at gunpoint and was facing serious time.

I spiraled out of control, but I was able to maintain for a while. As I had learned, I made sure to hide my use: a familiar burden. By 2016, when I woke up in the mornings, and before getting out of bed, I would do a shot of 100 mg of morphine. Soon I was doing heroin because it was cheaper. Of course I mixed it with meth so I could function, or so I thought. I lost my nice car, my nice job, my family, and my friends. All I had left was my house and my sweet little boy. I was an unfit mother and had him stay with his Grammy one night. She never let him return. After that, I literally walked out of my house and didn't look back: what good was my home without my son.

I became homeless. I was more alone, more lost, and more addicted. It seemed like this would be forever. I caught my first charge within a month and I found myself withdrawing, scared, and more alone that ever before in my empty jail cell. And that's where I encountered Jesus! I spent that whole month with Him in the cell. I felt I wasn't alone anymore!

I wish I could say it was all great from that point on, but it wasn't. An overdose, a couple more jail stays, a stint in rehab, and a 96-hour hold in the psych ward all followed over the next year.

Only by the grace of God, in January, 2018, I was supernaturally called to Freedom City Church! Immediately I felt his presence and felt so comfortable hearing the pastor share his background and preach about things I've never heard even talked about church. I knew why I had been called. I hadn't felt like I belonged in such a long time. I was "wrecked" by the love of God that day. I was saved that day and I finally began a new series in my life: a series of firsts.

It has been almost seven months since that day. I've been at Freedom City Church being discipled by our pastor and others through the Hope Home. It's the best thing that's ever happened to me besides my son. I'm thrilled to say that my relationship with my son and my dad is being restored. I haven't smoked a cigarette in those seven months and I just celebrated my eight month sobriety date! That doubles the longest time I've ever been clean and sober since I was 12. I owe it all to Pastor John, the Hope Home, all the wonderful people in my church, and most of all, God!

Today I don't hide behind anything. I don't feel like I have to lie about who I am: I can be me. In my weakness, He is my strength. I thank God for my trials and tribulations because He is with me and is preparing me for what's next in his divine plan. I also now know that the truth will indeed set you free!

Jason

I am very happy to share with you how I came to know my Lord and Savior Jesus Christ. The beginning of this journey began with the deaths of my wife, Amy, and my two-year-old son, Asher, in a car accident on June 16, 2014.

I had been an addict and alcoholic long before I met my wife. During the longest period of sobriety I had ever had, I met Amy and she had our son Asher. The day they were killed I immediately went back to doing drugs and the lifestyle that it entails. I blamed God and was so angry with Him. I remember praying to God saying, "I'll stay out of your business and You stay out of mine."

A little over a year later, 40 FBI agents raided my house and arrested me for drug trafficking and weapons charges. I was sentenced to 28 months in the federal correctional system. I was still very wild and lost, in every sense of that phrase.

After a fight I was in, I was sent to solitary confinement. I kept asking for books to read and finally one day the guards knocked on my door and told me someone asked for this book to be given to me. The book he handed me was Pastor John Alarid's book,

My Prison Became a Palace. I read it with tears flowing from my soul out through my eyes. I felt the pull of the Holy Spirit to talk to God. I got on my knees in that solitary cell in federal prison and asked God to save me from myself. What I felt is to this day indescribable! I felt new, a lightness had appeared in my soul that I had never felt before.

I asked for a Bible and what I read intrigued me and filled the hole that I had through the center of me for as long as I could remember. I couldn't get enough, I studied the Bible and read every book I could get my hands on that pointed to God and His character! All I wanted was to know Him better and to walk with Him as closely as possible. I continued studying and praying, everyday.

When I was released from prison, that first Sunday I went to Freedom City Church and found Pastor John. I needed him to know that his book, his testimony, led me to salvation in Jesus Christ. I have been attending CityReach, now called Freedom City Church, eagerly and faithfully every Sunday since. Pastor John and the entire Freedom City congregation have welcomed me with open arms and are guiding and mentoring me into what I believe with all my heart to be God's calling on me to be a Pastor. My life, the gift of my life through God's grace is more abundant than I ever could have thought or imagined! And it just keeps getting better everyday! I thank God for bringing me home to my family at Freedom City and I look forward to serving Jesus Christ alongside my brothers and sisters there!

I would like to conclude my story with my life Scripture, Hebrews 6:7: "For land that has drunk the rain that often falls on it, and produces a crop useful to those for whose sake it is cultivated, recieves a blessing from God."

My life has been the land that has drunk the rain of trials and hardships. But God is cultivating a spiritual crop that will be useful to those whom walk the same sin drenched path as I once did. I am excited to lead those who are lost in darkness to the Truth and the Light, Jesus Christ. Thank you for allowing me to give glory to my Father in heaven by sharing what Him and His grace have done in my life! May God bless and keep you and make His face to shine upon you!

Tom and Shelly

Tom: I've been a recovering alcoholic and have struggled with alcoholism my entire adult life. It's been extremely painful, especially for my wife, Shelly, and our four boys. I've caused a lot of suffering, pain, chaos, and deceit to those whom I love the most and this is something I will always regret as it's impacted our family in a negative way.

The early part of 2017, Shelly and I decided to separate and that involved big life changes; moving, selling many of our possessions, and both of us relocating into our own apartments. At this point in our lives, it was extremely painful and lonely for us and even though we separated we still considered ourselves married.

In the fall, I was suffering in my addiction and trying to figure out where to turn. I heard of a pastor on the north side of town who was a recovered heroin addict and was leading a church. One Sunday I decided I had nothing to lose and attended my first service at Freedom City Church. Pastor John Alarid was not preaching the first couple of Sundays I attended, but what I heard from the leadership and the people I was able to connect with, I knew this was a place for me.

On the third Sunday, Pastor John preached and he was on fire. The message had a strong impact on me immediately. It was also the first Sunday that pastor's book, *My Prison Became a Palace*, was for sale. I purchased a copy and went home and read the entire book that day. I decided to send a message to Pastor John to let him know I read his book and that I was an addict and his book really touched my heart. Pastor responded and asked if I would meet him for lunch. I was thrilled and so grateful for the invitation.

During lunch, Pastor John asked me to tell him my story so I did and let him know of my addiction and the suffering I and my family were going through. After lunch, we went to the car and he prayed over me. This was the first time I started to feel that there was hope for me, my marriage, and my family. One of the things he asked me to do was to get connected with Freedom City Church and start volunteering. Immediately, I found myself serving in the hospitality area and I did exactly what he asked me to do as he said, "It's not about me or the alcoholism; it's about God and serving people."

Several weeks later I was at home in my apartment going through the mail I received that day and I noticed a postcard, but it was addressed to John Alarid. At first glance I thought this was a fluke, but decided to take a picture of the postcard and send it to Pastor John. He messaged me back and said, "Do you live here?" I responded, "Yes sir I do." Pastor responded and said, "You can't make this kind of stuff up; this is all God." We discovered that not only do I live in the same apartment complex as Pastor did during his Bible college days, but I live in the exact apartment! Suddenly, it all came together for me and I began to weep: the separation and downsizing into our own apartments was God's way of leading me to meet Pastor John and to attend Freedom City Church.

Shelly: In January, 2018, I had heard a lot about Freedom City Church and the pastor so I decided to read his book. With the struggles Tom and I had been going through, and because I lost my older brother, Greg, to a drug addiction eighteen years ago, the book stirred up a lot of emotion. I was able to relate to some of the struggles Pastor John and his family faced through his years of addiction and the impact it has on a family.

Tom was invited to a Freedom City Church Dream Team dinner and asked if I would like to go with him. I decided to go along and was able to meet Pastor John and his wife, Hannah, along with several of the other leaders within the church. At this point, I figured I would just show up to church the following Sunday and see how my husband was serving and listen to the message. The biggest impact right away for me was the message Pastor John preached, and the way he taught the Bible so we could apply it to our lives today. I began serving alongside Tom every Sunday in the hospitality area. It's been a process, but the more we serve God the closer we feel to Him. Sometimes serving God takes us out of our comfort zone, but we now realize it's because God knows what He has planned and He is equipping us along the way so we are prepared.

Attending Freedom City Church we have realized that the slogan, "Reaching the One," means it doesn't matter what part of town you reside in or what kind of a job you go to every day. "Reaching the One" is for everyone and Freedom City Church is a place of worship for all to attend. We both look forward to serving together each week and even though we are still working through situations and still face obstacles, we are blessed, and full of happiness and joy! We are standing in faith knowing that one day we will be back together in the same house, but we are going to do it God's way!

We are thankful for our Freedom City Church family and will be forever grateful for the impact Pastor John and Hannah, as well as the rest of the leadership team, have made on our lives.

Zachary

For most of my life, I was a sold-out servant for Satan. When I was born I had already experienced heroin and who knows what other drugs because my mother and my father were both heroin addicts. My father was a member of a motorcycle club called the California Hessians. My mother was a One Percenters' wife (the One Percenters were known as the "baddest" of motorcycle outlaws.)

When I was two, my dad and my uncle were both gunned down on Thanksgiving day. Also, when I was two I was mauled by a pit bull and almost lost my ear. Throughout my life it seemed I was marked with a curse. Looking back, I now understand that many generational curses were attached to me. It is a miracle that I didn't die, existing in the situation I did. Drugs, gangs, and violence were normal parts of my life.

My major role models were criminals of every trade. Yes, I say trade because to me, as I was told, if someone was a professional shoplifter that was their trade. It was the same with grifters, prostitutes, and armed robbers.

When I was eight I was sexually molested. This caused me to sink into depression and anger. I started doing methamphetamine when I was eleven and became heavily involved with Neo-Nazi skinhead gangs. I spent my childhood and teen years in Lancaster, California, in Los Angeles County. I was kicked out of junior high and sent to a CDC program for organizing a youth skinhead gang in my school, and for possession of meth and sales of marijuana. I was heavily influenced by my older brother-in-law and firmly indoctrinated in hatred. I carried this hatred with me for many years.

When I was sixteen my mother decided she had enough of heroin and the never-ending cycle of being in and out of the LA county jail, and she also feared for my life. I was hanging out more and more with my brother-in-law who was a notorious member of the infamous prison gang, the Nazi Lowriders. She got me out by bribing me with meth to get me into her car and on the way to Missouri. Of course, it is common knowledge that a change of address does not change the person, so I continued with drugs, hatred, and a heart grown cold.

I began my prison career in the Missouri Department of Corrections in 2003. I was inmate 366902. I spent ten years incarcerated, which was most of my adult life. During that time I stayed focused on the darker side of things. I was heavily involved with the occult, specifically Odinism. In my prison time, I left my daughter fatherless.

Upon my release in 2007, I was determined to turn my life around. I started a business with a friend and began chasing the American dream. During this time, I gave up opiates, but ended up having major surgery for pleurisy. The doctors being good doctors got me firmly strung out again. But, instead of chasing the pills I decided to go the route of the methadone maintenance program. And, deception being deception, I believed I was in recovery. I had started attending a small Assemblies of God church in Crane, Missouri, because a business owner and a father in America takes his daughter to church! Something profound happened there: while praying I heard my friend's grandma speak in tongues and one of my friend's uncles give the interpretation. I don't even know why I was praying because I didn't believe. Then, I opened my eyes. The whole room was filled with a gold mist and it looked as if angels lined the pews. I knew this was real! So, when the pastor gave the salvation call I gave my life to the Lord and I was on fire for Jesus.

My background was Roman Catholic and I had been to funerals and weddings so I immediately started memorizing prayers, hail Marys, glory-be's, whatever. Instead of developing a relationship with God, I developed a religion. So, when the tragedies started coming, I quickly fell. My mom died of cancer and my business failed. I became self-destructive and I backslid into a form of apostasy. That was in 2010. When a man tried to kill me with a baseball bat, I beat him nearly to death and was charged with a class A first degree assault felony. That was Missouri's equivalent to attempted murder.

I sat in the Stone County jail facing thirty years and was fighting for my life. For nine months, I fought and finally snatched on a deal that I felt like I could do. I took a second degree assault charge and a seven-year sentence. I was filled with bitterness. Upon my release in 2015, I set out to play the catch-up game and become the baddest guy around. After seven months of daily meth use and alcohol and drug deals, I was charged again, this time with drug possession, gun possession, felonious restraint, and ACA. Fighting once again for my life, I was looking to game my way out in any way possible.

But, on Christmas Eve, I prayed. I cried out to God and He blessed me with a fear of the Lord. He removed his presence from me for only a split-second and I felt like an ancient piece of paper crumbling away. It was then that I begged for treatment which had never been offered to me before and I was sentenced to a year at Ozark Correctional Center in Fordland, Missouri. My walk truly began there. For that year, I sought the Lord and his face and He revealed Himself to me in miraculous ways. During that time, I was blessed with wisdom through the Word and I developed a passion for more of it. I was also blessed with a spiritual father who discipled me as I worked under him at the OCC chapel. Chaplain Marcink was a righteous, mad genius!

I attended services almost every night, held Bible studies, and prayed over every prayer request that was written. During that time, I was healed of gout, and that is documented. I was filled with the Holy Spirit with the evidence of speaking in tongues while praying over people at the prayer altars at Celebrate Recovery. And I was introduced to my general and pastor, John Alarid, pastor of Freedom City Church in Springfield.

I still remember the most influential words I will ever hear in my life. When thinking about going into the Freedom City Church Hope Home, I didn't want to do it. Who wants to give up relationships, not work a paying job, not have a cell phone, and not have other freedoms especially after being in prison as long as I was? I remember asking Pastor John, "What about my daughter? I need to be around her and take care of her." He looked at me dead in the eye and said, "Homie, how long have you been out of your daughter's life?" I told him it had been most of her life because I had spent most of my adult life in prison. He told me in words which rang true and floored me, "What's nine more months to never leave her again?"

So, I started praying. Later on, Chap Marcink told me he attended Freedom City Church as well. And then I had seen a friend of mine named Jason who I knew before we were both saved. He had saved my life on two occasions. It seems like I had a habit of fighting multiple people at once and Jason had been there twice to pull them off of me. He came walking into the prison one day telling me that he was the manager of the Hope Homes, and there is even more than that! I used to attend A.A. meetings in Branson West and I remember running into a man named Allan who would talk about how Jesus set him free from alcohol and who just happened to come preaching one day for

Freedom City Church, so I decided to take a leap of faith and go to the Hope Home. Also, during my time in OCC, I met a man who became my best friend, fellow prayer warrior, and soldier for Jesus Christ, David Manning. We both decided to go into the Hope Home.

During my time in the Hope Home, there were many trials and tribulations. But, during that time when I was about to leave to go and be with my daughter, God spoke to me through scripture. I didn't go and God restored my daughter to me by divine providence because I waited. Since then, the hand of God has always been on my life and I praise Him for it! I have graduated from the Hope Home and am now house manager at the Timothy House. I serve in Freedom City Church and am attending SUM Bible College and Theological Seminary. I work for Central Assembly of God.

God has blessed me to be in fulltime ministry after only a year out of prison with no formal education and a background like mine. I do not boast for it is all through the grace of God. I do rejoice for every trial and for every tribulation that my life has seen. It is our scars that mold us into oak and iron and it is the grace of God that opens doors. I now get to go back into the prison I left with my church to bring a message of hope, reaching the ones far from God with the gospel of Jesus Christ. I know the best is yet to come!

You Can be Set Free Too!

"God, our Savior . . . desires all people to be saved and to come to the knowledge of the truth" (1 Timothy 2:3-4).

The purpose of life is to be saved from sin (Romans 3:23, 6:23, 5:8, 10:9, 10:13), receive God's Holy Spirit (be born again, Ephesians 1:13-14), and become more and more like Christ Jesus every day (2 Corinthians 3:16-18). Each of us is part of God's plan. Once you are born again you will start to understand your role in the Kingdom: you will have renewed purpose and begin to walk in joyful obedience to God's call (Psalm 37:4).

When you say "the sinner's prayer" you are acknowledging God's plan of salvation for your life. There's no "magic formula" in praying the sinner's prayer, but if you pray it from your heart (Romans 10:8-11), God will send his Holy Spirit to live within you. You will know you are saved and set free!

The Sinner's Prayer

(Pray out loud, sincerely, from the heart)

Dear God, I confess I am a sinner, separated from You, and on my way to an eternity apart from You. I believe that your Son, Jesus, was born of a virgin and lived a sin-free life while He was on earth. He was fully God and fully man. I believe He was crucified and died in my place for my sins.

He was buried and resurrected on the third day.

He now sits on the right hand of God the Father in heaven.

I accept what you have done for me, Jesus, and believe I am forgiven of my sins.

I am set free!

John Caleb Alarid